Table of Contents

"A hospital bed is a parked taxi with the meter running."
-- *Groucho Marx*

SPECIAL THANKS

We want to acknowledge every person facing a health issue, as well as those people who are caregivers for someone dealing with health issues or special needs. We hope that in some way, our efforts in this book and at change:healthcare make dealing with the healthcare system just a little easier.

We went to some of the best people we know in the healthcare industry and asked them to add their voices to ours. They provided us with their comments, suggestions and stories. The result is what you are about to read.

Our most sincere thanks to each of these people for their contributions: Chris and Kim Blanz, Fred Eberlein, Chris Hartnett, Robert Henry, Von R. Glitschka, Fard Johnmar, Patsy Kelly, Steven Krein, Clayton McWhorter, Matt Mueller, Dr. Jay Parkinson M.D., Susan Sharpe, Dr. Scott Shreeve M.D., Unity Stoakes and Page Thompson.

We thank Hal Andrews, Chiara Bell, Frank Limpus, Dian Luffman, Christoph Milz, Will Rice and George Sibble for their invaluable feedback. We thank our wonderful interns Lauren Smith and Chad Boring, and publishers Tracy Lucas and Mary Catharine Nelson.

We also want to thank and recognize Townes Duncan, Will Fitzgibbon and Vic Gatto for their continued support.

1

GETTING YOUR BEARINGS

As Americans, we have been enjoying the all-you-can-eat buffet for some time. For decades now, that has also been our approach to healthcare. We pay for health insurance and assume that entitles us to whatever care we want, in whatever quantity we desire.

However, we've recently come to the rather rude awakening that many of us have been consuming too much – and that this is not necessarily the best for our long-term well-being. Our unlimited trips to the healthcare buffet have created an ever-increasing cost for our excesses. As premiums continue to rise, our employers cut back on what benefits we receive – they are taking some of the higher dollar items off of the buffet because they simply can't afford to pay for them anymore.

And there are discrepancies – serious ones – between those who have access to healthcare coverage and those who do not. Aside from the obvious, the costs and quality of care are often not equitable, and ironically they're not equitable among the insured either. It can be very tricky to tell who's paying whom for what and how much. Our healthcare system is difficult to understand and even harder to navigate.

Healthcare lacks *transparency*.

Transparency is what so many people are calling for today in the healthcare industry. When we say "transparency," we mean the idea that information regarding cost, quality, outcomes and experience should be readily available to all consumers of healthcare.

By making the healthcare industry more transparent, we as consumers will have a better idea of the true cost and quality of the care we receive, therefore making us more inclined to take responsibility and accountability for our own health.

If you or anyone close to you has ever been seriously ill, you already have more than a passing interest in healthcare. You've got a personal and probably a financial interest at stake. If so, that makes you a caregiver – a noble role and one that comes with a lot of responsibility.

If you read no further, know this: you have an advantage in dealing with the American healthcare system, whether you have insurance or you don't. Hospitals and doctors view their patients' bills in terms of DSO, or Days Sales Outstanding. HCA (Hospital Corporation of America), the nation's leading provider of healthcare services, measures DSO in *seconds*. Outstanding bills – patients' unpaid balances – are as important to them as they are to you. You have the money. The provider wants the money. That gives you, the healthcare consumer, the upper hand.

So, what do you do with this newfound realization of power? How do you deal with those medical bills, statements, collections notices and ceaseless phone calls? For starters, ditch that guilty

> *As my mother was declining in health due to cancer and I was trying to get my arms around all of her outstanding medical bills, I quickly realized upon calling her hospital and various doctors that they were much more eager to receive an immediate lump sum payment of a lesser amount than to receive full payment for the balance owed over a long period of time. I had forgotten that healthcare was also a business and just as in any other business,* ***cash flow*** *is king.*
>
> *-Christopher Parks*
> *change:healthcare*

feeling. **22% of people have been contacted by a collection service in relation to a medical bill**[1]**.** You're not alone. And with billing mistakes the way they are today, there's also a respectable chance that you don't owe the full outstanding debt. And if you do, there's a good probability you could arrange to pay less than the full amount.

So, here's the big secret when it comes to healthcare. We're laying it out here in the beginning, and even if you get no further than this point, this is the best tip:

Negotiate.

You have nothing to lose and much to gain if you pick up the phone and ask a doctor, hospital or any other healthcare service provider to accept less than what they billed you.

According to the January 2008 issue of *MONEY Magazine*, **60% of the consumers who asked their doctor or hospital for a discount on the account balances they owed did receive one in exchange for faster payment.**

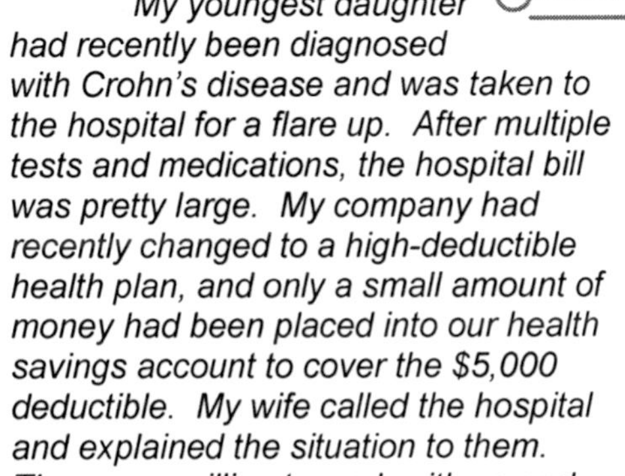

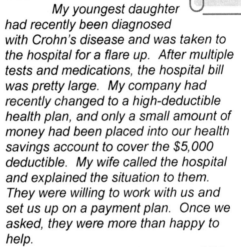

Hospitals Have Hearts Too

My youngest daughter had recently been diagnosed with Crohn's disease and was taken to the hospital for a flare up. After multiple tests and medications, the hospital bill was pretty large. My company had recently changed to a high-deductible health plan, and only a small amount of money had been placed into our health savings account to cover the $5,000 deductible. My wife called the hospital and explained the situation to them. They were willing to work with us and set us up on a payment plan. Once we asked, they were more than happy to help.

- Nashville Healthcare CEO

So, negotiate.

People in healthcare are not as picky as you might expect about the amount they get paid. In fact, they'll give you a better deal than you'd get from your local car dealer. The situation is

---

[1] USA Today/Kaiser Family Foundation/Harvard School of Public Health *Health Care Costs Survey* (Conducted April 25 – June 9, 2005)

different, of course. The car dealer can repossess your car as collateral. The hospital won't repo your pacemaker or re-break your leg. You have the leverage, not them. So, call up your provider and low-ball them. Go ahead. Offer them less than what you owe and offer to pay it promptly. Remember, every second that they delay accepting payment costs **them** money, not you.

So, let's push back from the healthcare buffet. Let's count the costs and see if we can gain some control over our excesses when it comes to healthcare. We've become more informed consumers on so many other fronts; homes, cars and electronics are just a few examples. **Now is the time to become better healthcare consumers, and this guide is your start.**

HOW TO USE THIS GUIDE

We hope this guide is pretty easy to understand and use. Defined words are in **bold**. These words can be found in the glossary at the end of the book. Because healthcare can be as unique as each individual, not every topic covered may apply to you or your specific circumstances. If something doesn't apply, feel free to skim forward until you reach a point where it does.

Breakout Boxes

Boxes like this provide you with a more in-depth understanding of the complicated and oftentimes more important aspects of healthcare.

There are Breakout Boxes with dotted line borders and an image of a big *. These boxes contain more information or highlight important aspects of the text. Read these for a more in-depth understanding.

We've also gotten input from some of the best and brightest people who are trying to change the healthcare industry for the better. Their stories and experiences are in the First Person boxes with the solid line border and the image of a patient. They give you an insider's look into what's going on in the healthcare industry.

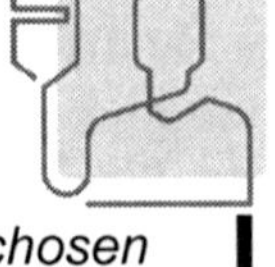

First Person

A lot of people have chosen to share their stories about dealing with healthcare. You'll find them quoted and referenced in boxes like these.

Sometimes we just can't help ourselves, and we jump up on a Soapbox to tell you about some of the greater injustices of the healthcare system; the issues that just can't remain the same. You won't get politics from us, but we think you'll agree, there are some pretty questionable things going on in the world of healthcare. These gray boxes with a person shouting are just our way of pointing out some of those gray areas.

At the end of each chapter, you'll find a list of Other Resources. These are some of the books, websites and other sources that we've found to be most useful.

Soapbox

We don't do it very often, we promise. But every once in a while, it just gets to be too much for us to bear, and we have to vent in boxes like this about the American healthcare system.

And finally, we'd be terribly hypocritical if we didn't give you, the consumer, the opportunity to provide us with feedback on what we're doing. So we do, and we make that information available to anyone who wants to read it. That's what transparency is all about.

This book is just the beginning. We'll take your comments and suggestions and show everyone our successes and failures as you see them. Visit *My Healthcare is Killing Me* online at **www.myhealthcareiskillingme.com**. We would love for you to share your stories and thoughts with us. We will post more stories, as well as updates about new developments in the industry. We will blog about more of the issues that could be in those gray soapboxes.

Information will also be available on the change:healthcare website. Go to **www.changehealthcare.com** to see more.

HOW TO USE THIS GUIDE: MAP

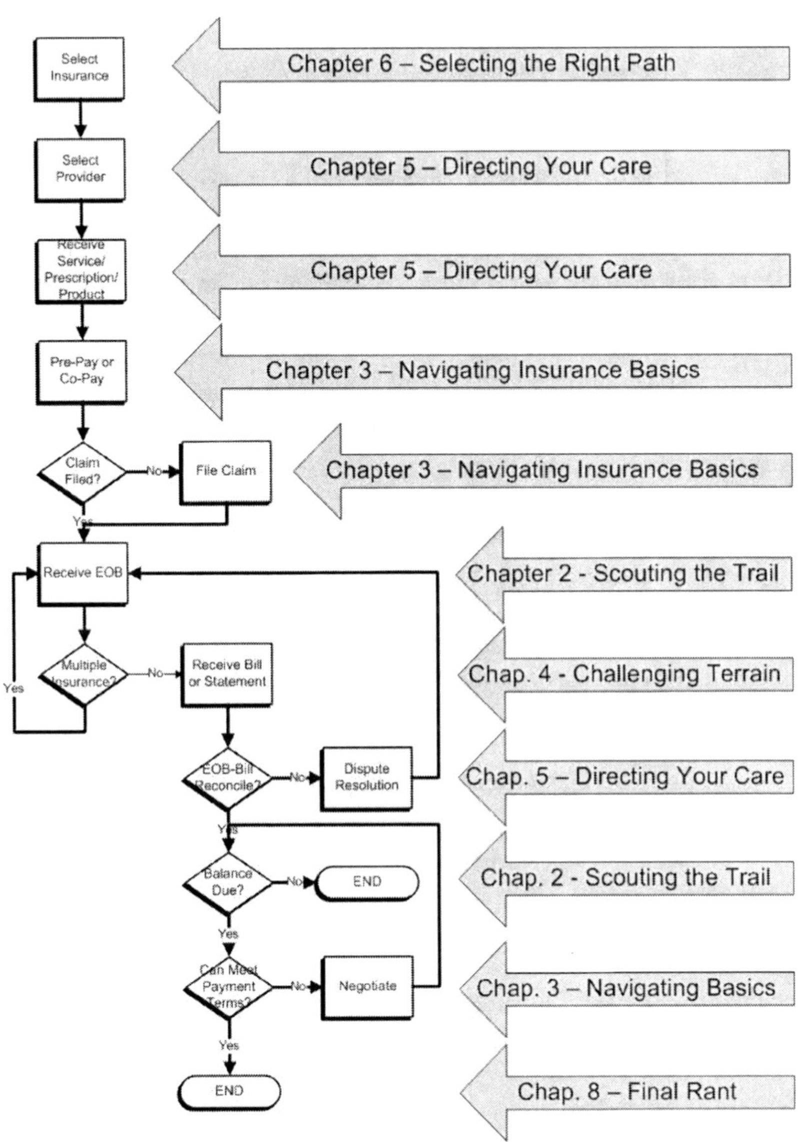

Select Insurance
Select Provider
Receive Service/ Prescription/ Product
Pre-Pay or Co-Pay
Claim Filed?
No
File Claim
Yes
Receive EOB
Multiple Insurance?
Yes
No
Receive Bill or Statement
EOB-Bill Reconcile?
No
Dispute Resolution
Yes
Balance Due?
No
END
Yes
Can Meet Payment Terms?
No
Negotiate
Yes
END
Chapter 6 – Selecting the Right Path
Chapter 5 – Directing Your Care
Chapter 5 – Directing Your Care
Chapter 3 – Navigating Insurance Basics
Chapter 3 – Navigating Insurance Basics
Chapter 2 - Scouting the Trail
Chap. 4 - Challenging Terrain
Chap. 5 – Directing Your Care
Chap. 2 - Scouting the Trail
Chap. 3 – Navigating Basics
Chap. 8 – Final Rant

A BRIEF HISTORY OF INSURANCE

Insurance is all about spreading risk. Modern day insurance companies have their origins in British firms who insured ships. Those early insurers looked at how many ships were being lost at sea. Based on that number, they knew that they'd lose a certain number of ships out of a group. They looked at the cost of the loss in terms of the value, and then they assembled a "pool" of ships to distribute the risk. They spread the cost of their expected losses over that pool and added a bit on top to cover the insurer's administrative costs and profits.

Healthcare insurance today works in much the same way. It's a far more refined process, of course, with lots of spreadsheets and much more data from years of collecting information. But at the heart of it all, insurers assemble a pool of people across which to spread the risk. Insurers calculate the expected losses and costs and divide that among the group. That's how they arrive at the **premium**, the amount paid to an insurer for coverage.

So, if you're in a pool with a group that has a lot of health issues, the insurance logically is going to cost the group more. If the health issues are few, the cost should be relatively less.

Higher Risk = Higher Cost

Health insurers are like the bookmakers in Las Vegas: both play the odds. They know how many winners and losers there will be. They know how many losers are needed to pay for their winners. Healthcare is the same way. If you hit the healthcare "house" big for a claim such as a heart attack or kidney transplant, the cost is being spread across all of the "losers" who paid more into their insurance than they got out. It's purely anecdotal, but we don't recall the last time that we saw a Las Vegas casino or a private healthcare insurer go broke.

2

SCOUTING THE TRAIL

Providers

Provider refers to the wide variety of medical professionals and service suppliers engaged in delivering healthcare-related products and services. The long list at the right of this page identifies some of the common and not-so-common types of providers, but is NOT comprehensive. Virtually any person or company who supplies a service or product related to healthcare can be considered a provider.

Providers

Anyone from whom you receive medical services or products is a provider. That includes:

- Doctors
- Nurses
- Hospitals
- Pharmacies
- Dentists
- Labs
- Medical Equipment
- Home Health Agencies
- Outpatient Clinics
- Ambulance Services
- Nurse Practitioners
- Physical Therapists
- Retail-Based Clinics
- Optical Shops
- Chiropractors
- Podiatrists
- Radiologists
- Psychiatrists
- Opticians
- Ophthalmologists
- And many, many more

Bills, Payments and EOBs

The majority of a person's interaction with their healthcare insurance comes in the form of **bills, payments** and **EOBs**, (or **Explanations of Benefits.**) Bills are sent by the **provider** to inform a patient of the expenses incurred. Payments are the money paid **out-of-pocket**. EOBs are sent by the insurer to inform patients about what items are covered, what adjustments the insurance company may have negotiated on the insured's behalf, what portion the insurer will cover and what the patient's payment responsibility will be.

Privacy and HIPAA

Your healthcare background is your personal information. For that reason, there is a federal legislation called the **Healthcare Information Portability and Accountability Act** (HIPAA) that determines how that information will be handled by medical professionals. There are often concerns that the information could be used to discriminate against someone in the workplace, in qualifying for insurance or in other ways. For that reason, your medical information is now guarded tightly by privacy policies in compliance with HIPAA. Any information about your health, including bills, payments and EOBs falls under HIPAA-regulated information.

Bills and Statements

A **bill** represents the dollar amount that a provider submits to your insurer (or charges you directly if you are uninsured) for **reimbursement** (payment) of a specific claim. A **claim** is a request for reimbursement typically submitted by your provider to your insurer in anticipation of receiving payment for their services. You may have to file your own claim with the insurance company if your provider does not do it for you. **Super bills** are bills that provide a line item detail of all the costs and services that make up a bill's total charges. A sample of a super bill appears on the following pages in Figures 1 and 2.

A bill is NOT what a provider will get paid. It is the MOST that a provider will be reimbursed. If there is no agreement between the provider and the insurer, the full billed amount is what the provider will attempt to collect. We'll discuss how that bill gets adjusted later, but be aware that even if you are uninsured, you should RARELY pay the original billed amount.

A **statement** is a summary of bills outstanding with a provider. Providers will send statements for a single bill as well. It can be easy to confuse a statement with a bill, but statements are generally clearly marked somewhere with the word "statement" and usually do not carry the same level of detail as a bill or super bill.

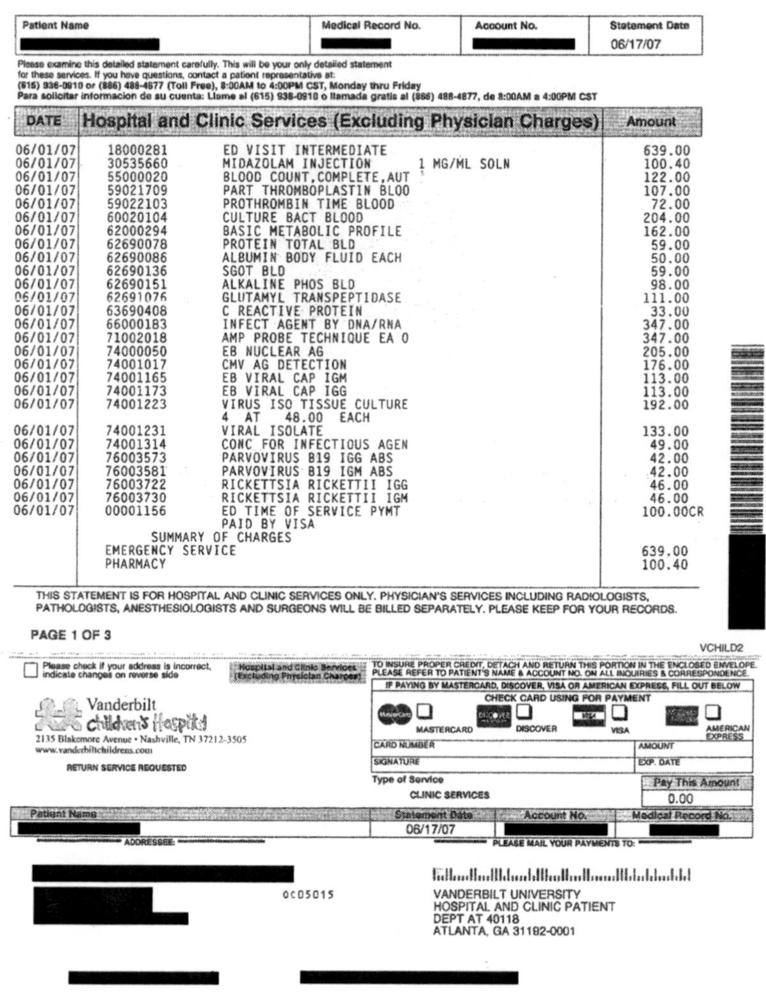

Patient Name	Medical Record No.	Account No.	Statement Date
			06/17/07

Please examine this detailed statement carefully. This will be your only detailed statement for these services. If you have questions, contact a patient representative at:
(615) 936-0910 or (886) 488-4677 (Toll Free), 8:00AM to 4:00PM CST, Monday thru Friday
Para solicitar informacion de su cuenta: Llame al (615) 936-0910 o llamada gratis al (866) 488-4877, de 8:00AM a 4:00PM CST

DATE	Hospital and Clinic Services (Excluding Physician Charges)		Amount
06/01/07	18000281	ED VISIT INTERMEDIATE	639.00
06/01/07	30535660	MIDAZOLAM INJECTION 1 MG/ML SOLN	100.40
06/01/07	55000020	BLOOD COUNT,COMPLETE,AUT	122.00
06/01/07	59021709	PART THROMBOPLASTIN BLOO	107.00
06/01/07	59022103	PROTHROMBIN TIME BLOOD	72.00
06/01/07	60020104	CULTURE BACT BLOOD	204.00
06/01/07	62000294	BASIC METABOLIC PROFILE	162.00
06/01/07	62690078	PROTEIN TOTAL BLD	59.00
06/01/07	62690086	ALBUMIN BODY FLUID EACH	50.00
06/01/07	62690136	SGOT BLD	59.00
06/01/07	62690151	ALKALINE PHOS BLD	98.00
06/01/07	62691076	GLUTAMYL TRANSPEPTIDASE	111.00
06/01/07	63690408	C REACTIVE PROTEIN	33.00
06/01/07	66000183	INFECT AGENT BY DNA/RNA	347.00
06/01/07	71002018	AMP PROBE TECHNIQUE EA 0	347.00
06/01/07	74000050	EB NUCLEAR AG	205.00
06/01/07	74001017	CMV AG DETECTION	176.00
06/01/07	74001165	EB VIRAL CAP IGM	113.00
06/01/07	74001173	EB VIRAL CAP IGG	113.00
06/01/07	74001223	VIRUS ISO TISSUE CULTURE 4 AT 48.00 EACH	192.00
06/01/07	74001231	VIRAL ISOLATE	133.00
06/01/07	74001314	CONC FOR INFECTIOUS AGEN	49.00
06/01/07	76003573	PARVOVIRUS B19 IGG ABS	42.00
06/01/07	76003581	PARVOVIRUS B19 IGM ABS	42.00
06/01/07	76003722	RICKETTSIA RICKETTII IGG	46.00
06/01/07	76003730	RICKETTSIA RICKETTII IGM	46.00
06/01/07	00001156	ED TIME OF SERVICE PYMT PAID BY VISA	100.00CR
	SUMMARY OF CHARGES		
	EMERGENCY SERVICE		639.00
	PHARMACY		100.40

THIS STATEMENT IS FOR HOSPITAL AND CLINIC SERVICES ONLY. PHYSICIAN'S SERVICES INCLUDING RADIOLOGISTS, PATHOLOGISTS, ANESTHESIOLOGISTS AND SURGEONS WILL BE BILLED SEPARATELY. PLEASE KEEP FOR YOUR RECORDS.

PAGE 1 OF 3

VCHILD2

☐ Please check if your address is incorrect, indicate changes on reverse side

Hospital and Clinic Services (Excluding Physician Charges)

TO INSURE PROPER CREDIT, DETACH AND RETURN THIS PORTION IN THE ENCLOSED ENVELOPE. PLEASE REFER TO PATIENT'S NAME & ACCOUNT NO. ON ALL INQUIRIES & CORRESPONDENCE.

Vanderbilt Children's Hospital
2135 Blakemore Avenue • Nashville, TN 37212-3505
www.vanderbiltchildrens.com

RETURN SERVICE REQUESTED

IF PAYING BY MASTERCARD, DISCOVER, VISA OR AMERICAN EXPRESS, FILL OUT BELOW
CHECK CARD USING FOR PAYMENT
☐ MASTERCARD ☐ DISCOVER ☐ VISA ☐ AMERICAN EXPRESS

CARD NUMBER	AMOUNT
SIGNATURE	EXP. DATE

Type of Service
CLINIC SERVICES

Pay This Amount
0.00

Patient Name	Statement Date	Account No.	Medical Record No.
	06/17/07		

ADDRESSEE:

0C05015

PLEASE MAIL YOUR PAYMENTS TO:

VANDERBILT UNIVERSITY
HOSPITAL AND CLINIC PATIENT
DEPT AT 40118
ATLANTA, GA 31192-0001

Figure 1: Page 1 of a Super Bill for $3,667

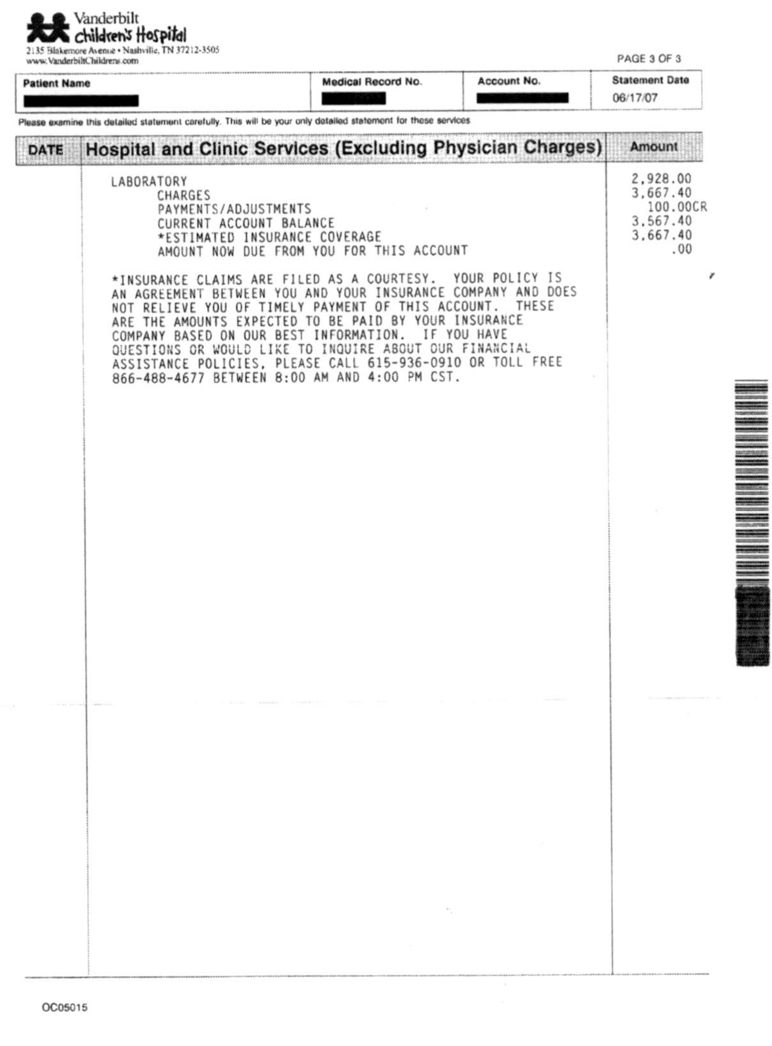

Vanderbilt Children's Hospital
2135 Blakemore Avenue • Nashville, TN 37212-3505
www.VanderbiltChildrens.com

PAGE 3 OF 3

Patient Name	Medical Record No.	Account No.	Statement Date
[redacted]	[redacted]	[redacted]	06/17/07

Please examine this detailed statement carefully. This will be your only detailed statement for these services

DATE	Hospital and Clinic Services (Excluding Physician Charges)	Amount
	LABORATORY	2,928.00
	CHARGES	3,667.40
	PAYMENTS/ADJUSTMENTS	100.00CR
	CURRENT ACCOUNT BALANCE	3,567.40
	*ESTIMATED INSURANCE COVERAGE	3,667.40
	AMOUNT NOW DUE FROM YOU FOR THIS ACCOUNT	.00

*INSURANCE CLAIMS ARE FILED AS A COURTESY. YOUR POLICY IS AN AGREEMENT BETWEEN YOU AND YOUR INSURANCE COMPANY AND DOES NOT RELIEVE YOU OF TIMELY PAYMENT OF THIS ACCOUNT. THESE ARE THE AMOUNTS EXPECTED TO BE PAID BY YOUR INSURANCE COMPANY BASED ON OUR BEST INFORMATION. IF YOU HAVE QUESTIONS OR WOULD LIKE TO INQUIRE ABOUT OUR FINANCIAL ASSISTANCE POLICIES, PLEASE CALL 615-936-0910 OR TOLL FREE 866-488-4677 BETWEEN 8:00 AM AND 4:00 PM CST.

OC05015

Figure 2: Page 2 of a Super Bill for $3,667

Payments –
Not Everybody Pays the Same Amount

For identical services, your provider will *bill* you the same amount that they billed everybody else. But what you actually pay can be different from what many other people paid. That's because your **provider** has negotiated (there's that word again) with your insurer to *accept* a pre-determined amount. So, the amount you'll pay ultimately depends on the contract negotiated by your insurer.

Billed versus Allowed

The Billed Amount is the amount your provider charged. The Allowed Amount or Negotiated Rate is the amount that they have agreed to accept based on a contractual agreement with you or your insurer. Since those amounts vary depending on the deal they have structured with different insurers, that rate varies. So usually, the Billed Amount is higher than the Allowed Amount. That way, the provider maximizes what they get reimbursed by billing above the maximum amount allowed by their contract. This can be as much as ten times actual cost!

That's because the buying power and negotiating abilities of your insurance company determine the price paid for the service. Insurers negotiate based on the volume of insured members they have – a larger number of insured members generally means a higher discount can be negotiated. It's an issue of **billed amount** versus **allowed amount** or the **negotiated rate** (see the breakout box).

Again, we'll make the comparison to the car dealer. Think of the billed amount as the MSRP (Manufacturer's Suggested Retail Price). People don't pay that amount. They negotiate, and they don't wind up paying the same thing that someone else paid for an identical car at the same dealership. Healthcare is similar, except that your insurer has already set the price on your behalf. You don't pay MSRP; you pay what your insurer has negotiated by virtue of the volume of patients they will direct to that provider.

Where you are geographically can play a role in determining price, too. In areas with more than one provider, like larger metropolitan cities, there are more options and therefore some competition that results in an option for better pricing (price elasticity). In areas with few options, like rural areas, it's a sort of monopoly. You can't go anywhere else, the provider knows it and negotiating price is not as easy (the price is inelastic).

If you are uninsured, what you are being billed for your healthcare services is the equivalent of being billed MSRP for your car. Knowing the average allowed amount, or negotiated rate, of the healthcare services you received gives you a good idea of the price you **should** be paying. This average negotiated rate lets you know how much your provider typically gets reimbursed for the services provided. As an uninsured patient you are basically paying MSRP for your healthcare. Consider all the additional money you pay as icing on the cake for your provider. Doesn't make much sense, does it?

> To find out more information on average allowed amounts for services and providers visit www.changehealthcare.com or check out DataiSight's consumer website at www.ncnconsumerconnect.com

EOBs

If you have insurance, you may receive an **Explanation of Benefit**, or **EOB**, and it may arrive even before the bill. The EOB shows you what the doctor billed.

The EOB also shows you what the insurance company will *allow* the doctor to receive (the allowed or reimbursed amount), what the insurance company paid and your payment responsibility as the patient. On the example EOB in Figure 3, subtract the network savings from the submitted charges to arrive at the *allowed* amount of $358.

The EOB tells most of the story because it describes how the money is going to flow. The first key piece is the allowed amount that the doctor ultimately is going to be paid (or reimbursed). Remember, the billed amount from the doctor is like the MSRP (Manufacturer's Suggested List Price or the "sticker price") on a car. Nobody with any sense pays that. Your insurer has negotiated a better rate and that's the **allowed amount**.

Different insurers may call it the **allowed rate, contracted amount, covered charges** or **adjusted rate**. But, ultimately, it's the total amount that the provider winds up being paid (again, or reimbursed, in insurance lingo). The money comes from your insurance company and/or your payments.

We've provided a few sample EOBs on the following pages and highlighted the important pieces of information as a point of reference.

THIS IS NOT A BILL

It's an EOB or Explanation of Benefit, and just about all of them state THIS IS NOT A BILL in big bold letters.

EOBs are important, however. They show you what the insurance company has negotiated on your behalf with your provider. They show you what your insurer agrees is a fair rate. And they show what has been paid and what part of the bill is going to be your responsibility.

An Independent Licensee of the Blue Cross and Blue Shield Association

BlueCross BlueShield of Tennessee
801 Pine Street
Chattanooga, Tennessee 37402

DATE: 07/04/2007

EXPLANATION OF BENEFITS

Summary of BlueCross BlueShield of Tennessee, Inc. Claim Processed on 07/04/2007

Claim Number: [redacted] Received 06/19/2007 Group Number: [redacted]

Identification No: [redacted]
Patient Name: [redacted]
Date Services Provided: 06/01/2007
Provider Name: VANDERBILT CHILDRENS HOSP

If you have questions about this statement, please call
1-800-422-6712
or visit Member Self-Service at our web site at www.bcbst.com to view this information and more.
Chattanooga 8:00 A.M.-5:15 P.M. (ET)
Memphis 8:00 A.M.-5:15 P.M. (CT)
Monday - Friday

SUMMARY

Total Charge Submitted	3,667.40
Total Benefits Provided/Network Savings	3,567.40
Other Insurance Benefits	.00
Amount You Owe Provider (Contact your provider if you receive a bill for more than your EOB indicates that you owe.)	100.00

THIS IS NOT A BILL

ITEMIZATION OF CHARGES

Date of Service	Services Included	Submitted Charges	Network Savings	Deductible Amount	Coinsurance if Applicable	Copay if Applicable	Non-Covered	Notes	Paid Provider
06/01/07	Hospital Outpatient Services	3,667.40	3,309.40			100.00			258.00
	TOTAL	3,667.40	3,309.40			100.00			258.00

ACCOUNT STATUS

AT END OF DAY 07/04/2007 FOR THE YEAR 2007:

	IN-NETWORK	OUT-OF-NETWORK
This individual has now paid the following amounts toward DEDUCTIBLE:		$ 225.05 Family

	IN-NETWORK	OUT-OF-NETWORK
This individual has now paid these amounts toward OUT-OF-POCKET MAXIMUM:	$ 200.00 Individual	$
	$ 200.00 Family	$ 225.05 Family

You have the right to appeal the results of this claim. If your plan is subject to the Employee Retirement Income Security Act of 1974 (ERISA), the appeal must be submitted within 180 days of this Explanation of Benefits. Under ERISA you may file a civil action after the appeal decision. Please refer to the appeals section of your Evidence of Coverage or contact Customer Service.

Page 1 of 2

Thank you for allowing us to serve you. Please visit our Web site at www.bcbst.com

Figure 3: The EOB for the Super Bill for $3,667 showing that the Billed Amount was reduced to a Negotiated Rate of $358 – of which the insurer paid $258 and the patient paid $100

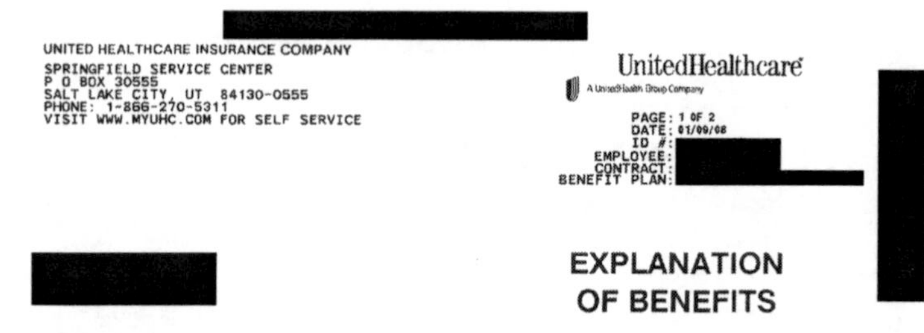

UNITED HEALTHCARE INSURANCE COMPANY
SPRINGFIELD SERVICE CENTER
P O BOX 30555
SALT LAKE CITY, UT 84130-0555
PHONE: 1-866-270-5311
VISIT WWW.MYUHC.COM FOR SELF SERVICE

UnitedHealthcare
A UnitedHealth Group Company

PAGE: 1 OF 2
DATE: 01/09/08
ID #:
EMPLOYEE:
CONTRACT:
BENEFIT PLAN:

EXPLANATION OF BENEFITS

SERVICE DETAIL

PATIENT/RELAT CLAIM NUMBER	PROVIDER/ SERVICE	DATE OF SERVICE	AMOUNT CHARGED	NOT COVERED	AMOUNT ALLOWED	COPAY/ DEDUCTIBLE	PLAN COVERS	BENEFIT AVAILABLE	REMARK CODE
	CH TIC OFFICE VISITS	09/16/07	59.00		59.00	59.00		0.00	W1
		TOTAL	59.00		59.00	59.00		0.00	
						PLAN PAYS		0.00	
						** PATIENT PAYS		59.00	
	CH TIC OFFICE VISITS	09/16/07	59.00	59.00				0.00	TQ
		TOTAL	59.00	59.00				0.00	
						PLAN PAYS		0.00	
						** PATIENT PAYS		0.00	

** DEFINITION: "PATIENT PAYS" IS THE AMOUNT, IF ANY, OWED YOUR PROVIDER. THIS MAY INCLUDE AMOUNTS ALREADY PAID TO YOUR PROVIDER AT TIME OF SERVICE.

REMARK CODE(S) LISTED BELOW ARE REFERENCED IN THE "SERVICE DETAIL" SECTION UNDER THE HEADING "REMARK CODE"
(W1) THESE EXPENSES HAVE BEEN APPLIED TO THE PATIENT'S ANNUAL DEDUCTIBLE. THE PATIENT IS RESPONSIBLE FOR PAYING THE PHYSICIAN OR OTHER HEALTH CARE PROFESSIONAL ALL CHARGES THAT ARE APPLIED TO THE ANNUAL DEDUCTIBLE PLEASE FORWARD THIS PAYMENT TO YOUR PHYSICIAN OR OTHER HEALTH CARE PROFESSIONAL.
(TQ) THIS CLAIM HAS ALREADY BEEN PROCESSED AND THE ALLOWABLE AMOUNT WAS APPLIED TO THE YEARLY DEDUCTIBLE. THE PATIENT IS RESPONSIBLE FOR PAYMENT TO THE PHYSICIAN OR HEALTH CARE PROFESSIONAL.

SATISFIED 2007 TO DATE	IN NETWORK DEDUCTIBLE	IN NETWORK OUT OF POCKET	OUT OF NETWORK DEDUCTIBLE	OUT OF NETWORK OUT OF POCKET
FAMILY	$500.00	$226.64	$59.00	$534.00
CH	$500.00	$226.64	$0.00	$0.00
PLAN YEAR 2007	FAMILY: $1000.00 INDIV: $500.00	FAMILY: $4000.00 INDIV: $2000.00	FAMILY: $2000.00 INDIV: $1000.00	FAMILY: $8000.00 INDIV: $4000.00

A REVIEW OF THIS BENEFIT DETERMINATION MAY BE REQUESTED BY SUBMITTING YOUR APPEAL TO US IN WRITING AT THE FOLLOWING ADDRESS: UNITEDHEALTHCARE APPEALS, P.O. BOX 30573, SALT LAKE CITY, UT 84130-0573. THE REQUEST FOR YOUR REVIEW MUST BE MADE WITHIN 180 DAYS FROM THE DATE YOU RECEIVE THIS STATEMENT. IF YOU REQUEST A REVIEW OF YOUR CLAIM DENIAL, WE WILL COMPLETE OUR REVIEW NOT LATER THAN 30 DAYS AFTER WE RECEIVE YOUR REQUEST FOR REVIEW.

YOU MAY HAVE THE RIGHT TO FILE A CIVIL ACTION UNDER ERISA IF ALL REQUIRED REVIEWS OF YOUR CLAIM HAVE BEEN COMPLETED.

* * * * * * *

YOU CAN MEET MANY OF YOUR NEEDS ONLINE AT WWW.MYUHC.COM. AT ALMOST ANYTIME DAY OR NIGHT, YOU CAN REVIEW CLAIMS, CHECK ELIGIBILITY, LOCATE A NETWORK PHYSICIAN, REQUEST AN ID CARD, REFILL PRESCRIPTIONS IF ELIGIBLE, AND MORE! FOR IMMEDIATE, SECURE SELF-SERVICE, VISIT WWW.MYUHC.COM.

HOW TO REGISTER?
YOU CAN REGISTER AND BEGIN USING MYUHC IN THE SAME SESSION. ACCESS WWW.MYUHC.COM TO REGISTER. THE INFORMATION REQUIRED IS ON YOUR INSURANCE ID CARD (FIRST NAME, LAST NAME, MEMBER ID, GROUP NUMBER AND DATE OF BIRTH).

* * * * * * *

FURTHER EXPLANATION OF BENEFITS INFORMATION IS ON CONTINUATION PAGE(S)

THIS IS NOT A BILL

Figure 4: This is an EOB from United Healthcare. If you compare it to the EOB in Figure 3, you will notice the differences in language and how the information is presented.

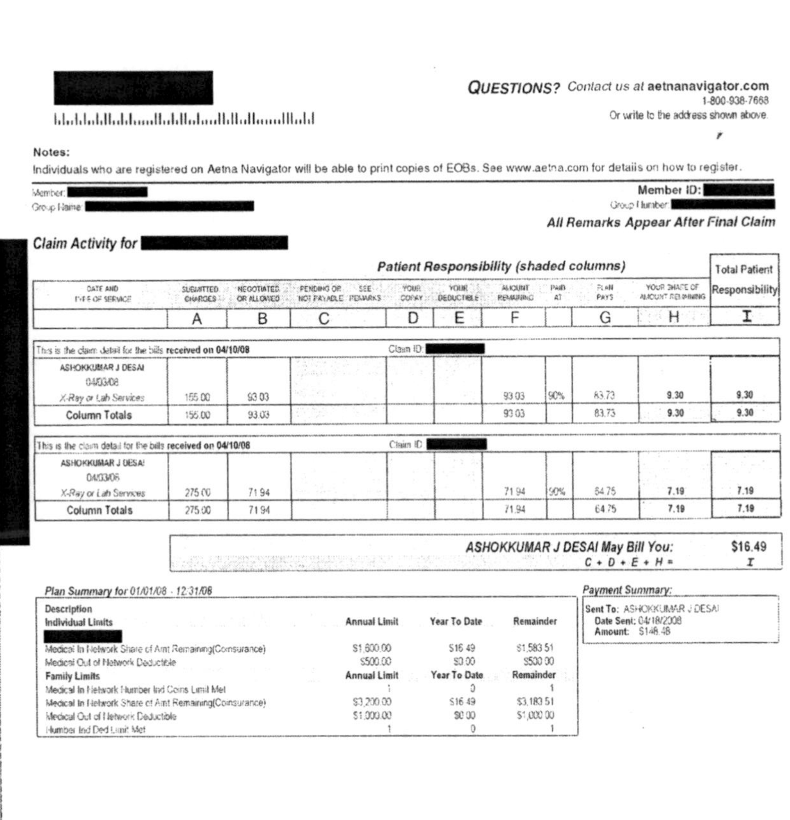

Aetna

Aetna L[illegible]surance Company
P.O. [illegible] 14079
LEXINGTON, KY 40512 4079

EXPLANATION OF BENEFITS

THIS IS NOT A BILL

Please Retain for Future Reference
Date Printed: 04/23/08
Page 1 of 1

QUESTIONS? *Contact us at* **aetnanavigator.com**
1-800-938-7663
Or write to the address shown above.

Notes:
Individuals who are registered on Aetna Navigator will be able to print copies of EOBs. See www.aetna.com for details on how to register.

Member:
Group Name:

Member ID:
Group Number:

All Remarks Appear After Final Claim

Claim Activity for

Patient Responsibility (shaded columns)

DATE AND TYPE OF SERVICE	SUBMITTED CHARGES	NEGOTIATED OR ALLOWED	PENDING OR NOT PAYABLE / SEE REMARKS	YOUR COPAY	YOUR DEDUCTIBLE	AMOUNT REMAINING	PAID AT	PLAN PAYS	YOUR SHARE OF AMOUNT REMAINING	Total Patient Responsibility
	A	B	C	D	E	F		G	H	I
This is the claim detail for the bills **received on 04/10/08**				Claim ID:						
ASHOKKUMAR J DESAI 04/03/08 *X-Ray or Lab Services*	155.00	93.03				93.03	90%	83.73	**9.30**	**9.30**
Column Totals	155.00	93.03				93.03		83.73	**9.30**	**9.30**
This is the claim detail for the bills **received on 04/10/08**				Claim ID:						
ASHOKKUMAR J DESAI 04/03/08 *X-Ray or Lab Services*	275.00	71.94				71.94	90%	64.75	**7.19**	**7.19**
Column Totals	275.00	71.94				71.94		64.75	**7.19**	**7.19**

ASHOKKUMAR J DESAI May Bill You: **$16.49**
C + D + E + H = *I*

Plan Summary for 01/01/08 - 12/31/08

Description			
Individual Limits	**Annual Limit**	**Year To Date**	**Remainder**
Medical In Network Share of Amt Remaining(Coinsurance)	$1,600.00	$16.49	$1,583.51
Medical Out of Network Deductible	$500.00	$0.00	$500.00
Family Limits	**Annual Limit**	**Year To Date**	**Remainder**
Medical In Network Number Ind Coins Limit Met	1	0	1
Medical In Network Share of Amt Remaining(Coinsurance)	$3,200.00	$16.49	$3,183.51
Medical Out of Network Deductible	$1,000.00	$0.00	$1,000.00
Number Ind Ded Limit Met	1	0	1

Payment Summary:

Sent To: ASHOKKUMAR J DESAI
Date Sent: 04/18/2008
Amount: $148.48

Figure 5: This is an EOB from Aetna. If you compare it to the EOB in Figures 3 and 4, you will notice the differences in language and how the information is presented.

Virtually all medical bills that are insurance-mediated claims can be broken down into four components. Those components are the billed amount, the discount amount, the amount that insurance paid and the patient responsibility. The percentages for each claim may be different (we'll get into that a bit later), but the components of the bill remain the same.

Some EOBs present only the amount of the discount, or the network saving, and not the **allowed amount**. They prefer to place the emphasis on how much they "saved" you. You might need to grab a calculator to figure out what the provider was allowed – just take the billed amount and subtract the discount.

Billed Amount

– Discount Amount

= Allowed Amount

Some insurers give you the full math. They show you the discount and then show you the resulting allowed rate and any non-covered charges.

Billed Amount

– Discount Amount

= Allowed Amount

– Insurance Paid

= Patient Responsibility (Including Non-Covered Charges)

Unfortunately, there is no set standard among insurance companies, and they are left to their own devices to determine how to best present your EOB to you. This can result in confusion amongst consumers due to inconsistencies from different insurers' use of terminology. The chart on the following page shows you a sampling of some of the various terms we've found that insurers use on their EOBs.

EOB Terminology

We've seen lots of EOBs. Lots. And each one is unique, right down to the terms they use. Here's a quick reference list so you can try to match yours with ours:

Billed Amount	**Adjustment**	**Allowed Amount**	**Insurance Paid**	**Patient Responsibility**
Charged Amount	Network Savings	Amount Allowed	Provider Payment	Amount You Owe
Provider Charge	Discount	Payment Amount	Amount Paid	Patient's Responsibility
Amount Billed	Provider Discount	Allowable Amount		Your Minimum Responsibility
Amount Charged		Remaining Covered Charges		You Are Responsible For:
Charge		Contracted Amount		Estimated Member Responsibility
Charged Amount				Amount You Owe to Provider
Total Charges				Patient's Minimum Responsibility Owed to Provider
				Patient Pays

In summary, paying the full amount for what a provider bills is generally like paying sticker price for a car. Nobody should pay MSRP for a car, and you shouldn't pay MSRP for your healthcare either, whether you're insured or not.

So how do you get the best rate? Be informed, do a little research on the cost of services you received, and then use your knowledge to your advantage.

Are We Willing to Change?

When it comes to healthcare, Americans are a study in contradictions. According to research produced in early 2008 by the Mayo Clinic and Harris Interactive, many people are deeply concerned about rising health expenses. 91% percent of respondents said health costs are too high.

In fact, those making more than $75,000 annually were most likely to complain about the cost of their care. Despite this, most people are unwilling to take basic steps to squeeze every penny from their health dollar. Most want no limitations on the care they receive. In addition, they have no interest in conducting research to ensure they are getting the highest quality treatment. The Mayo/Harris study revealed that 70% of respondents believed that care should be based on patients' preferences rather than cost.

- Fard Johnmar
Founder, Envision Solutions

Other Resources

American Academy of Family Physicians produces a website that has resources for men's health, women's health, individuals interested in healthy living and an Over-the-Counter Guide. Visit them at **www.aafp.org**

FamilyDoctor.org, a website from the American Academy of Family Pysicians, even provides Health Tools and a Smart Patient Guide, which includes information on choosing a family doctor, understanding your medical bills and much more.

Patient Advocate Foundation is a national not-for-profit organization that helps patients diagnosed with life-threatening or debilitating diseases by guiding them through effective communication to assure their access to care, maintenance of employment and financial stability. Additional information is available at **www.patientadvocate.org**

Medical Billing Advocates of America offer a website with a variety of resources to help you with your medical bills. Most importantly, if you need a person to help you, the website has a tool that allows you to search for a billing advocate in your own area.

Many insurance company websites offer guides to understanding your EOB online. Search the web for your insurance company and tools to help you better understand your EOB.
www.billadvocates.com

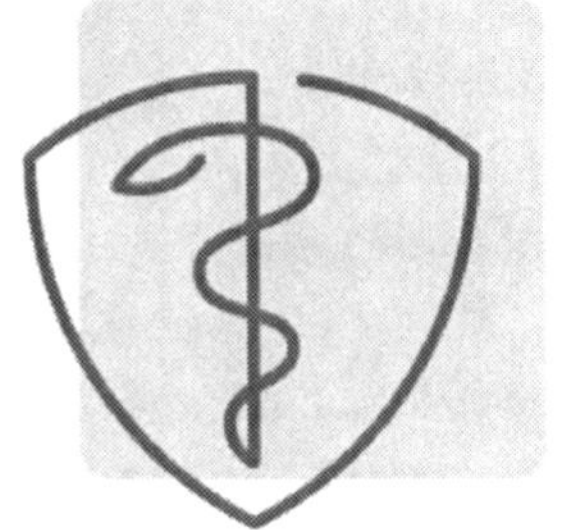

3

NAVIGATING INSURANCE BASICS

The Network

When health insurance companies have existing contracts with **providers,** those providers are then considered to be "**in-network**." That means that the doctors, hospitals or other providers have agreed to accept a **negotiated rate** for their services. That negotiated or **adjusted rate** is the allowed amount.

Deductible

The amount that you have to pay out of your own pocket toward healthcare services before your insurer starts to pay for covered services is known as your deductible. That is the number you are told about when you first enroll in your plan. It's a very specific figure that generally ranges from $500 to $5,000 and affects the cost of your monthly premium. And for most people, this is a figure that they don't wind up dealing with, so they don't give it another thought. However, if you have any major medical services beyond a basic office visit, your deductible is very important. It is the portion of the healthcare expenses you are initially expected to pick up.

The provider is obligated by contract to accept that negotiated or adjusted rate.

In-Network

An insurer is a **guaranteed payor** to **in-network** providers. That means that the insurance company assures payment of the expenses incurred on your behalf to that provider. Since your insurer has guaranteed through their contract that they will pay for all covered services, when you go in for an expensive procedure, the provider does not have to ask you to go through a credit check as you would when buying a car. To put it in perspective, the cost for open-heart surgery can easily surpass $30,000, but your surgeon does not generally run a credit check on you. That's because when you present your insurance card, they know that an insurer stands behind you as a guaranteed payor for that service, assuming that the services are necessary and covered under your benefits plan.

There are exceptions, of course. If you are about to receive a treatment that is not covered, then you may be asked to sign a **promissory note** or secure credit in some way. This is a common practice when procedure is not covered or if a procedure or treatment is considered "experimental" as with some cancer treatments.

If there is any question about whether a treatment or procedure is covered, it is best to get **pre-authorization**.

Self-Pay or Cash-Pay

Oftentimes when you are out-of-network, you will find that providers will ask you to self-pay or pay in advance. This is also referred to as cash-pay (even if payment is made via a check, credit card or other form of payment). Many dentists require self-pay these days. Dental benefits have suffered as one of the earliest casualties as benefits have been steadily reduced in an effort to control costs.

Providers often will know which procedures may not normally be covered and may require pre-authorization. They may even initiate the authorization process on your behalf with your insurer. However, in some cases, they may not and that can leave you with the bulk of the expense – and leave the provider expecting payment from you as the patient. It is the patient (or insured's) responsibility to know when a pre-authorization is necessary.

Out-of-Network

When an insurer has no contract with a provider, the provider is considered **out-of-network**. That means there is no negotiated rate between the insurer and provider, and all bets are off. This also means that you may be asked to pay the billed amount – the equivalent of the MSRP. Oftentimes, non-participating providers will not file a claim for you. So, you may have to file a claim with your insurance carrier yourself to see if they will cover any of the services. Each insurance company will have its own procedure for out-of-network a claims. In the worst case, your insurance may not pay for the services at all. However, they may instead pay a percent of the total billed amount, or they may pay only up to the amount they would have paid for the service to an in-network provider and leave you with the responsibility for the balance. It's up to you to check and be sure that you are using an in-network provider for any healthcare services you receive. The

When In-Network is Out-of-Network

It is common for hospitals to be in-network, yet still use additional service providers who are out-of-network. That can leave you stuck with a larger-than-expected bill. For example, your hospital may be in-network, but the anesthesiologist used may not be. If so, and you had no say in the selection of that out-of-network provider, then you may not be responsible for paying the out-of-network charge.

back of your insurance card should have information on where to find coverage and claims information. When in doubt, visit your insurance company's website or call their 800 number on your card or EOB.

If you use an out-of-network provider, you would be well advised to seek a more favorable negotiated rate than what they may present initially. Go ahead and haggle. The worst they can do is say "no." But chances are good that they'll be more than willing to give you some kind of discount in exchange for timely payment.

If your provider is not in your insurer's network, they may have a negotiated rate with a different insurer – a negotiated rate which the provider is willing to accept. It is difficult to know exactly what that rate might be. However, you can begin to get an idea through research. Medicare is the federal government insurance that covers the more than 44 million Americans of retirement age (and growing as the boomers enter the Medicare ranks). Medicare payments serve as a baseline for negotiated rates. The full set of CMS (Centers for Medicare and Medicaid Services) reimbursement rates are available to the public through many Internet sites. Start by taking a look at **http://www.cms.hhs.gov/ PhysicianFeeSched/**

Private Insurance & Federal/State Insurance

Healthcare insurance can be broken into four major categories – privately insured, federally insured and uninsured.

- **Private insurances** are policies offered through an employer or an individual policy.
- Sometimes, people who have insurance are **underinsured** and find themselves facing the same situations as those who are completely uninsured when coverage is denied.
- **Federal/State Insurances** are Medicare, Medicaid and TRICARE. Some states offer a state plan, but that is generally a supplement to one of the federal plans, and they vary so much and so often that any information presented here would be quickly outdated.
- **Uninsured** are without **coverage** of any kind.

The government leverages their number of insured to receive a volume discount. It also helps that, as a government entity, federal legislation rather than market forces set their rates.

No matter how much or how little your insurance covers, we can't say it enough, especially if you are uninsured. **Negotiate.** Haggle. If the bill creates a financial burden, you are not comfortable with the amount or you're simply trying to save money, call up and make an offer. You have the money. They want it. Use that to your advantage. Ask what sort of discount you can receive if you pay promptly.

Co-Pay

The fee you pay on initial rendering of services, generally a set fee, is the **co-pay**. $20 is a common amount for an office visit. A co-pay at the emergency room may be closer to $100, but it still is a co-pay.

The intent of the co-pay is to make us as consumers invest a nominal fee before utilizing our healthcare. The theory is that the co-pay serves to give a consumer pause before using their healthcare insurance frivolously. However, the side

The $20 Office Visit

Many Americans have developed the attitude that a doctor visit costs only $20. They have equated the immediate outlay at the doctor's office to the expense of the visit. That is NOT the case. The co-pay is simply a mechanism meant to deter unnecessary healthcare use. However, the American healthcare consumer has been conditioned to associate the co-pay amount with the cost of the visit because he or she is so far displaced from the total cost paid. Imagine taking your car in for every scratch, broken piece of trim or new wiper blades and charging it to your insurance. Your rates would go through the roof. Healthcare is insurance, too – you just use it more than you do your auto insurance. The more you use it, the more your rates go up.

effect of that small fee has trained us to perceive the cost of services as the cost of the co-pay. And so, when we talk with people and ask if they know what the cost of an office visit is, they generally reply with the amount of their co-pay. That is NOT the actual cost of the visit.

Take a look at the chart below that shows who pays for healthcare. It breaks apart the co-pay from the rest of the billed amount. Now you can begin to see that it takes at least three different payments before a provider sees the entirety of their services reimbursed.

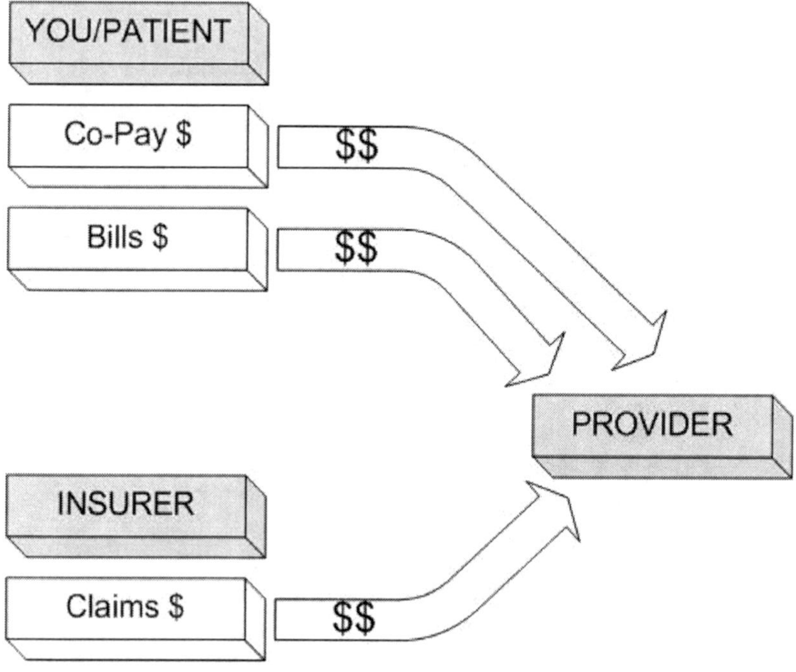

Provider Reimbursement Chart – It can take three different instances before a provider receives full reimbursement.

Most basic office visits begin at around $45 and can run $200 or more in major metropolitan areas.[2] The balance above your co-pay is picked up by your insurance and ultimately passed on to your employer, who is looking to shift more of the financial burden to us as consumers with the goal of having us be more responsible for our own healthcare. So in the end, the premium goes up, which makes the amount that you must contribute go up. It's like buying now with no payments for a year, but the interest accruing while you wait. Eventually, it catches up to you, as it is right now with so many Americans and their employers.

Deductible

The amount you are expected to pay for your health insurance out of your own pocket is the **deductible**. The deductible is one of the more difficult concepts in healthcare to nail down because there are so many nuances from one policy to another. Going back to the car example, if you break a windshield, you may have to pay a $100 deductible before the insurance company will cover the remaining cost.

The deductible on your health insurance functions in a very similar way. However, it is important to understand what the deductible is NOT. The deductible is NOT the maximum amount you will be expected to pay out of your own pocket for your healthcare in a given year.

Typically the deductible is **NOT** the maximum amount you can expect to pay out of your own pocket for your healthcare in a given year. Rather it represents the amount you are responsible for paying before your insurance carrier begins to cover a greater percentage of service costs.

[2] Girion, L. (2006, September14) Study Says Individual Insurance Too Costly. The L.A. Times. Accessed on 02/20/2008. http://tinyurl.com/6nd9wn

Basically, the deductible represents the amount that you are expected to pay for medical procedures during the course of your coverage year *before the insurance company starts paying.*

Deductible in Detail

Your EOB generally tells you when a payment applies to your deductible. Once you meet your deductible, your insurance company picks up your healthcare expenses according to your co-insurance (that's the 90/10, 80/20 or 100% option selected for your plan).

Your deductible resets each year on renewal of your insurance. So on a calendar year policy, each January, any expenses you have had during the previous year that counted toward your deductible are wiped away, and you are on the hook again for the full amount of your deductible.

Under some policies, your co-pay may count toward your deductible. However, as insurers look for ways to continue making the profit they need to keep the insurance in place (with minimal premium increases), it is increasingly rare that co-payments count toward the deductible. There is simply no hard and fast rule.

By way of example, if you have a $10,000 procedure in a year wherein you have no other payments that count toward your $5,000 deductible, you may expect to pay $5,000 and have your insurance pick up the $5,000 balance.

But there's another wrinkle. **Co-insurance.**

Co-Insurance: 80/20, 90/10 or 100%

Co-Insurance is how you and your insurer split the balance of the reimbursement amount after the deductible has been met. If you have a 100% co-insurance plan, you can skip this section, go and hug your employer, tell them you love them and will never leave them. The rest of you, read on.

Using the previous example, after you've paid the $5,000 deductible of your $10,000 bill, there's still more to pay that will be your responsibility. If you have a 90/10 co-insurance plan, you will have to pay 10% of the remaining balance, or in this specific case, $500. Your insurance picks up the other 90%. If you have an 80/20 plan, you have to pay 20% of the remaining balance, or $1,000. Your insurance picks up the other 80%.

$15,000 Out-of-Pocket for New Parents

"I have twin daughters. They were born early and spent 28 days in the NICU (Neonatal Intensive Care Unit) and ran up a bill of $250,000 at birth. We were fortunate and had good insurance. Our out-of-pocket expense came to $15,000. That's tough for new parents to take. So, we called up the hospital NICU administrators and asked what they could do to help. They had already received payment from the insurer, so our money was only icing on the cake for them. They graciously reduced our amount to the $3,500 we had already paid and wrote off the rest. All we did was ask. No haggling at all. We just asked."

- Robert Hendrick
change:healthcare

Now, take that one step further and up the ante on your bill. On an extensive hospital stay with a $100,000 bill, you might have the initial $5,000 plus 10-20% of the $95,000 balance. That's an additional $9,500-19,000 that is your responsibility. That brings total out-of-pocket to $14,500-$24,000.

Now that's a reason to negotiate! Even if you have insurance you can still negotiate further, but only after the provider's fees have been knocked down to negotiated rates.

So call up and ask. Have we said that it pays to negotiate?

Maximum Out-of-Pocket Expense

Your policy should have a **maximum out-of-pocket expense,** or a **stop-loss amount**. This is the most that you will be expected to pay for health services during the course of the year. However, be aware that those amounts, just like your deductible, start over again each year. Be sure not to confuse maximum out-of-pocket with maximum lifetime benefit, which is the point at which your insurance will have paid all they are going to pay and will turn the remainder over to you regardless of the stop-loss amount. For more about **maximum lifetime benefit**, see Chapter 5.

Why So Much Paperwork?

One simple visit to a provider can result in a mountain of paperwork. There are bills, statements and EOBs. And not just one set, but bills, statements and EOBs from people and places you've never heard of, much less had anything to do with directly. Who are these providers and why are they sending bills?

Whom Do I Call to Negotiate?

When you receive a bill from your provider, there should be a phone number for their billing department included. This is a great place to start. Remember that the provider must bill everyone the same amount for their services. However, they are able to except different payments amounts. The specialists in the billing department are generally experienced and directed to negotiate payments. Some facilities are even required to provide uninsured patients the same price as their best-negotiated rate.

Many people don't ask. They just wait until the smoke clears to see who still hounds them for money after the insurance gets done paying for things. They let the bills go all of the way or almost to the point of collection attempts before acting to pay them.

A single doctor's office usually can't provide all the care you require for an episode of treatment. However, more often than not, the dramatic increase of bills and EOB paperwork has resulted from a growing trend amongst providers to specialize in certain types of healthcare services, as well as the guidelines used by the government and insurance companies to determine what and how services shall be reimbursed.

There are tests to be run, scans to be made and services to be performed. Some of those services require specialists to be brought in. A simple outpatient surgery or trip to the ER can generate numerous encounters with different providers, resulting in separate bills being sent to the patient.

When Confusion Comes After the Care...

In December of 2006, our son was admitted to the hospital for a very rare condition that turned out to be treatable, but scary and stressful nonetheless. My wife and I will be eternally grateful for everything everyone in the hospital did for us. The doctors, nurses, technicians, cafeteria workers, janitors, receptionists, parking garage attendants, security guards, etc., all deserve a medal for what they did for our family. On second thought, forget the medal... they should be granted sainthood. Everyone played their part perfectly.

On the other hand... although our insurance helped keep us from bankruptcy, the entire insurance system is in desperate need of an overhaul. It is complex, bureaucratic and downright confusing. We continued to get bills for months after he was released. If it is this confusing for us as consumers, I can only imagine the nightmares the doctors go through in just trying to get paid.

- Chris Blanz
Founder, Cabedge

Consider a typical outpatient surgery. Here's how it might break down:

- Facility
- Specialists
- Lab
- Lab Technician
- Anesthesiologist

There are 5 different providers, each with a potential bill and EOB. That's 10 pieces of paperwork. When the statement arrives, that number of ten gets pushed to 15. If you have secondary insurance, make it 20 pieces of paper to keep up with, organize or (like most people tend to do) simply ignore. Wait another month (go ahead, most people do anyway), and 5 more statements show up – increasing your medical paperwork pile to the equivalent of short paperback novel.

Paperwork Piles Up

"Remember my twin daughters and their $250,000 birth? That one event generated over 500 pieces of paper. It was like having three people in the hospital at once, and we did. There was paperwork for my wife, the first child and the second child – each one billed as a separate individual. We had more than a ream of paper!"

- Robert Hendrick
change:healthcare

With an ER visit, it may be even worse:

- Ambulance
- Doctor
- Specialist - Surgeon
- Imaging

- Labs
- Lab Technicians
- Facility
- Anesthesia

And that's just for starters – 8 providers with an EOB, a bill and a statement make for at least 24 pieces of paper.

And don't forget the follow-up care after the fact, such as lab work and physical therapy, which will generate even more paperwork.

The following image further emphasizes the amount of paper that is generated when visiting a provider and the number of different instances in which money changes hands in healthcare.

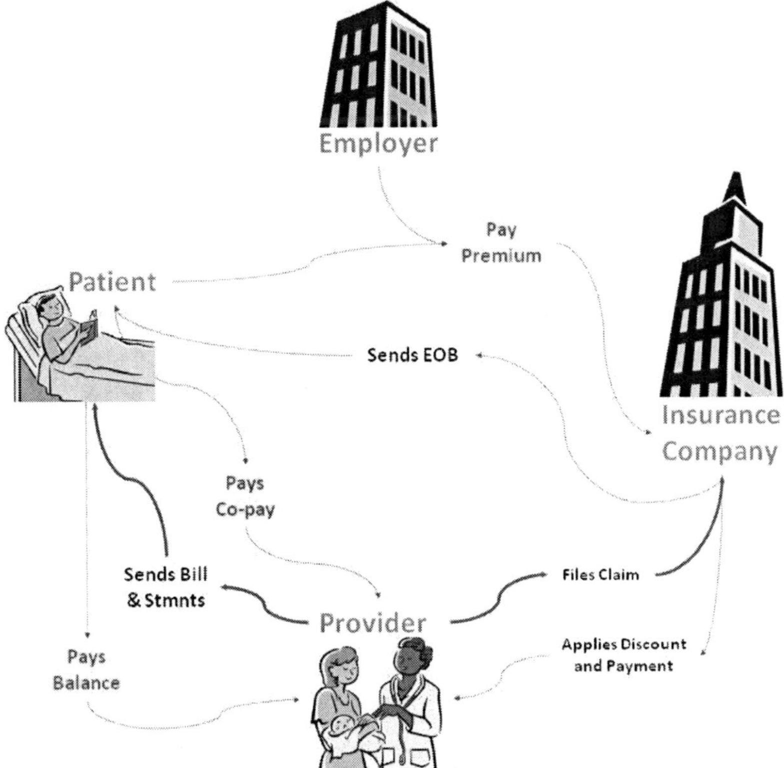

Healthcare Paper and Dollar "Flow Chart"

Where to Start Negotiating a Medical Bill

If you know what someone else has paid, then that could be your starting point. But simple negotiating tactics teach that the best place to start is with the lowest offer – and **Medicare** provides just that information.

Medicare is the government-sponsored healthcare program for retirees. They have lower negotiated rates than commercial insurance because they have the largest group of customers (think buying power). They have 44 million Americans age 65 and up. People need healthcare as they get older, so Medicare not only has lots of people, but higher usage rates. Add to that the 42 million on **Medicaid** and the 9 million American veterans (and their families) eligible for **TRICARE**, the federal government comprises the largest guaranteed payor in the American healthcare market. That gives them heavy buying clout! Not to mention that they get to set their rates by legislation rather than negotiation. They simply tell the providers what they are going to pay by law.

Regional and Severity Adjustment

Medicare rates are adjusted both by region and by severity. Providers in regions of the country where people earn more generally receive a higher reimbursement rate. In more rural areas, you may see a lower rate, though that generalization does not always hold true.

Severity adjustment refers to the fact that not all hospital admissions are created equal for the same health issue. One hospital patient's admission for a heart attack compared to that of another heart attack patient that also has diabetes or some other complicating health issue will require more time, attention and services than the non-complicated heart attack patient. The severity adjustment helps to determine roughly how costly a procedure is and reflect an appropriate "multiplier" for reimbursement. Think of it as a batting average. A 1.0 is really average. A 1.2 severity means that the instance of severity is 20% worse. A 0.8 means it is 20% less.

As a result, the lowest rates are almost always the Medicare/Medicaid rates, and as a government entity those reimbursement rates are a matter of public record. So, if you want to find the best price point at which to start negotiating, look no further than the Medicare reimbursement rates.

Many of the negotiated-rate contracts that insurers have with providers are based on Medicare fee schedules plus a certain percentage that the insurer will pay above the baseline Medicare rate. With over 40,000 different services and treatments for which providers might bill, it is too time consuming for a provider to negotiate each of them on an individual basis. As a result, most providers and insurers use the Medicare fee schedules as a baseline, and depending on their degree of leverage, the negotiated rate is a percentage above the Medicare rate. If a provider has a "center of excellence" (i.e. a stroke, heart, oncology, burn center etc.), that facility might carve out that specialty to receive a slightly higher reimbursement rate in recognition of its emphasis on providing focused or "higher quality" care within that particular specialty. Therefore true centers of excellence, or specialty institutions that provide a niche service, negotiate a higher reimbursement rate because they are the only provider in their region who is able to deliver those services.

Cost-Shifting

With the government representing the largest payor in the country, when they make changes in the reimbursement rate for procedures, it obviously has far-reaching implications. Periodically, the government will actually reduce its reimbursement rates on certain procedures or services. When it does, however the cost of the procedure remains the same, so providers have to make up the lost revenue somewhere. And they have nowhere to go, but the privately insured market. The effect is known as cost-shifting. So when you hear of Medicare rates going down, just know that it could mean your private insurance rates are going to go up to compensate.

The data is thick, but there are a number of websites that break the rate down into plain English (or at least something close). Check out changehealthcare.com for a range of the most current negotiated rates accepted by providers, including most major services and pharmaceutical standard reimbursement rates. The rates vary by region and by severity.

Change in Healthcare

There is a movement going on in healthcare because people like you and me are demanding new solutions. And we're not only making demands, we're doing something about it. We're creating new businesses. We're researching our options. We're arming ourselves with knowledge. We're taking the mystery out of what has been a con game for far too long.

- Unity Stoakes
President and Co-founder
OrganizedWisdom.com

Other Resources

Centers for Medicare & Medicaid Services information is provided as part of the federal government's Health and Human Services Department. This is the site for all things related to Medicare and Medicaid and can be found at **www.cms.hhs.gov**

Vimo.com helps consumers comparison shop for their health. You can purchase health insurance plans, find doctors in your area, compare hospital procedure costs and find over-the-counter prescription medications.

Revolution Health is a consumer-centric health company focused on transforming the way people approach health and wellness. Visit **www.revolutionhealth.com**.

WebMD provides health information and tools to manage your health. The site also provides support to individuals seeking additional health information. To find out more, visit **www.webmd.com**

Intuit offers its Health product for tracking medical bills. We're understandably biased toward our own Medical Bill Management service at **www.changehealthcare.com**, but we're not afraid to let you know what else is out there. This helpful tool can be found at **www.intuit.com**

The website at **www.changehealthcare.com** has all the tools you need for managing your medical bills, payments and EOBs as well as information on reimbursement rates for Medicare and private insurance.

Printed Materials

Navigating Your Health Benefits for Dummies provides clear and concise information on what you need to know about health benefit. [Cutler, Charles M., MD, MS, and Tracey A. Baker, CFP. Navigating Your Health Benefits for Dummies. Indianapolis: Wiley. 2006.]

Health Insurance Resources – A Guide for People with Chronic Disease and Disability is a great resource guide for individuals with chronic health conditions or disabilities. This book would also be useful to anyone attempting to better understand the healthcare system. [Northrop, Dorothy E., MSW, ACSW, Stephen E. Cooper, and Kimberly Calder, MPS. Health Insurance Resources - A Guide for People with Chronic Disease and Disability. New York: Demos Medical Publishing. 2007.]

4

MORE CHALLENGING TERRAIN

Negotiated Rates

Providers agree to be reimbursed at negotiated flat rates because they are willing to play the odds that in the long run, they will win more than they lose. That works in their favor sometimes, other times not. It is not uncommon for an ER visit to run thousands of dollars, yet the reimbursement to be only a few hundred.

For example, a local hospital prided itself on being the number one

$3,667 equals $358

I took my youngest child to the ER and ran up a bill of $3,667 before the visit was complete. It was classified as a Level 1 ER visit, and my insurer had negotiated a flat rate of $358 for a children's Level 1 ER visit. I was essentially at the all-you-can-eat ER buffet line, and they lost money on me. But these are odds makers – so, they made it up on someone who came in with a splinter or some less cost-intensive option, or on a hapless uninsured who would have actually been expected to pay the $3,667 bill that only hit my insurance for $258 and me for the $100 ER co-pay.

- Robert Hendrick
change:healthcare

hospital for delivering babies. They had agreements with insurers that paid them a fixed amount per uncomplicated birth. Those **capitated contracts** caused them to lose $200 per child delivered. They bore (no pun intended) that cost with the hope of securing the mother's and her family's major medical needs for years to come based on a good initial experience with the hospital. Birthing babies was their loss leader.

Four-Dollar Prescriptions

A lot of the large retail pharmacy chains have gone to the $4 prescription. And it's about time they came clean. Some of the prescriptions for which they're charging only $4 were only $4 or less to begin with. If you had a $20 Rx co-pay, they often took the $20 co-pay you gave them and pocketed the extra dollars as pure profit. While that practice has largely ended, it does not bode well for building a relationship based on trust and transparency.

And for prescriptions that are more than your co-pay, those $4 prescriptions may still be billed to your insurance if you have it. If your co-pay was $10 for a $50 generic, the pharmacy gets your $4 and might still get the $40 balance from your insurance. So, they still take in $44 for the $50 prescription.

Prescriptions

Prescriptions are an area of healthcare where transparency is particularly lacking. The prescription you buy at one pharmacy is not the same price at the competitor down the road. In fact, prices can vary 40% within the same metropolitan area. They can even vary as much as 20% within a chain in a major metropolitan area[3]. Your prescription plan co-pay may be the same, but the total price paid by your insurer may not be the same. It's not uncommon to find that a prescription that costs a total of $120 in one pharmacy may be $80 literally a few doors down.

[3] change:healthcare inc. (2007). *Case Study: Pharmaceuticals Cost Variances.* Retrieved July 21, 2008, change:healthcare inc. Website: http://company.changehealthcare.com/blog

If you have a Health Savings Account (HSA), High Deductible Health Plan (HDHP), are uninsured, are receiving medication that is not covered, or are otherwise going to be personally responsible for your out-of-pocket expense on prescriptions, you should shop around for the best price. Even if you have insurance and your insurance covers 100% of the cost above your co-pay, if you frequent a pharmacy that gets a higher rate for prescriptions, you are contributing to the rise in healthcare premiums for you and your employer. Your tendency to go to a higher-priced pharmacy will get factored in when the insurance is underwritten the following year. If you buy expensive medications now, you'll pay for them later with higher premiums. Unfortunately, often with prescriptions you don't know what the price was to begin with.

The Long-Term Impact of Using Your Insurance

The risk associated with each insured group is taken into account when premiums are established. This is called underwriting. Initially, underwriters make assumptions based on past historical data, usually self-reported survey data supplied by individuals to the insurer. Over time, the underwriters develop a more accurate picture of the frequency and usage of the group's healthcare. They adjust the rates when it comes to renewal time based on that information. And according to the Millman Report, those rates increased an average of 7.6% from 2007-2008.

Pharmaceuticals are the cash cow of the healthcare industry. Trying to figure out what was billed, what was allowed and how much you should actually pay is a challenge and a chore.

One major chain proudly prints on their prescription packages "Your insurance saved you $X dollars." Wrong. Your insurance did not "save" you that amount. The pharmacy simply charged you a certain amount and was reimbursed the balance through your insurance company.

Our own research confirms these pricing discrepancies. We did a survey of local pharmacies, all within the local metropolitan area of a city with around 1 million inhabitants. We called and asked for pricing on specific prescriptions and explained that our insurance would not cover the prescription, and we needed to get retail pricing. The results were surprising. There was an average 20% variation in the retail prices! For more expensive drugs like Copaxone (used for treating symptoms of Multiple Sclerosis) that difference ranged between $1,890 and $2,276.09 a difference of $386.09 a month! If you factor in low-cost online service providers such as drugstore.com, the variation becomes even more widely pronounced.

By the way, that prescription co-pay may not be such a good deal anyway. If your insurance encourages you toward generics as most do, you may be overpaying, because many

Reorganizing Drug Plans

Unfortunately, economic and policy trends are forcing consumers to become much more informed and cost-conscious. Industry players have instituted a number of reforms designed to shift the financial burden from third-party payors like government and employers to individual patients. In April 2008, the *New York Times* reported that insurance firms have begun to abandon the traditional arrangement in which patients paid a fixed amount (usually between $10 and $30) for costly drugs.

Today, some patients pay a percentage of the total cost for a medication. For example, a person taking a drug with a monthly tab of $1,900 would have previously paid $20. After the policy change, they would be required to pay $325. Surprisingly, the government, not private health insurers, first introduced this policy. Medicare insurance plans regularly require some patients to pay a percentage of their total prescription medicine bill.

- Fard Johnmar
Envision Solutions

generic prescriptions cost far less than the co-pay. The pharmacy *may* simply charge you the full co-pay and pocket the rest as pure profit.

So, why do some stores charge so much more? Convenience. Consistently, chains with the corner stores offered the highest prices. Convenience costs more. And as a healthcare consumer, that's your prerogative to take advantage of the more convenient option. Ultimately, though, your premiums will pay for that choice. If not this year, then next year when your group is underwritten again.

Quality Versus Cost

Our next point may shock you. Generally speaking, high quality healthcare often costs LESS than low quality healthcare. No, that's not a misprint. But that does not mean that price always determines quality. Here's why.

Poor quality healthcare can be defined as healthcare that fails to get you the appropriate diagnosis and treatment on the first visit. Studies have shown that the chance of getting the right diagnosis and treatment from your provider on the first visit is 50%.[4] You may even get the right diagnosis, but a less than adequate treatment regimen. Let's face it, healthcare isn't easy; and it's getting more complicated all the time. There's a reason it takes eight years or more of higher education to become a medical doctor.

A Pennsylvania government survey of the state's hospitals that perform heart bypass surgery highlights the idea that high cost healthcare is not indicative of high quality healthcare. Of the hospitals surveyed, the best-paid hospital received about $100,000 on average for the operation while the lowest-paid hospital received less than $20,000. The kicker here is that both hospital

---

[4] Bass, S. *How Important is Diagnosis?* Retrieved July 23, 2008, from Super Nutrition & Superior Health Website: http://drbass.com/diagnosis.html

patients had similar lengths of stay and comparable mortality rates. Though the hospitals had several "excuses" for the differences in cost, the survey and New York Times article[5] clearly highlight the growing trend that cost is NOT necessarily representative of the quality of care provided.

This concept can also be seen with non-surgical procedures and treatment. For example, the care for a pneumonia patient who receives the proper diagnosis and treatment the first time, stands to cost significantly less than a patient who does not initially receive proper diagnosis and treatment. This patient may remain in a lower quality hospital several days longer than a patient who received higher quality care. Factor in the cost of lost work days and quality of life, and the cost of the poorer quality provider is potentially many times more than that of the higher one.

What causes the difference? It could be any number of factors. Failure to make the appropriate diagnosis. Failure to assess the severity of the illness. Failure to prescribe appropriate treatment. Poor record keeping by hospitals and other providers. Or any combination of those factors. The bottom line is – *higher quality healthcare* ***can*** *cost less than poor quality healthcare.*

Going back to our example of the car from the local dealer, the car now has a dent in the fender. If our auto shop worked like healthcare, here's how the repair might play out:

We take our car to the repair shop. They pull the dent, charge us and send us home. We look at it and decide that the dent is still there and now the paint is flaking, so we take it back. The body shop throws on some Bondo and repaints the fender. Looks good at first glance. We pay again. A few days later it becomes apparent that the fender is still not quite right, and now the condition is worsening because it's starting to rust. We've

---

[5] Abelson, R. (2007, June 14). In Health Care, Cost Isn't Proof of High Quality. *New York Times*. Retrieved August 4, 2008 from www.nytimes.com.

already paid for the first two repairs, and now the body shop tells us that what we need is a new fender. We have to pay for a third time. Like the poor quality provider, the poor quality body shop costs us much more than if we had paid the better body shop at the start and simply gotten the appropriate service. Meanwhile, we lost access to our car for many more days while the repairs were repeatedly made. Even if there were no additional charges, we lost time and the use of the car.

Ridiculous, right? But this is exactly how healthcare works. For example, a patient went to a doctor for a pain in the shoulder. The doctor prescribed a strong anti-inflammatory and said, "If that doesn't do the trick, then I'll send you to a shoulder specialist." Its always good to hear that there are options other than surgery, so let's assume that the anti-inflammatory was less invasive and far less costly than surgery, but was it the right treatment? Should the patient have skipped the cost of the anti-inflammatory and the cost of a follow up visit, and gone straight to the shoulder specialist where he was likely to wind up anyway?

Insurers and providers have good reason and generally good intentions to encourage the lower costing and less invasive methods of treatment first. Doing so may hold down costs in the short-term, but long-term financial ramifications are less clear. And since most private insurance relationships rarely last more than 2-3 years, it could be argued that the insurance companies are not focused on the long-term.

In the end, these choices are your prerogative as an informed and responsible healthcare consumer. However, now you can see why it pays to be up to speed on healthcare issues instead of blindly trusting choices solely to your physician or insurance company.

Multiple Insurances

Some people are fortunate enough to be covered by more than one insurer – they have a primary and a secondary insurer. While such situations are more common among Medicare enrollees, it also occurs among privately insured. For example, both spouses may have insurance through their respective employers, one of them on a family plan for dependents while the other spouse holds an individual policy.

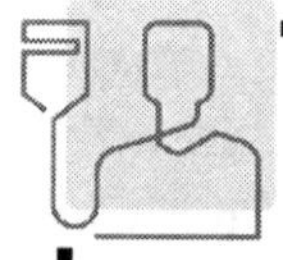

Enough Insurance for Three

Many Americans who have reached the retirement age enjoy the advantage of more than one insurance. My parents have three. Their primary insurer is Medicare. Their secondary is a Blue Cross/ Blue Shield supplemental policy, and my father as a veteran of the National Guard has TRICARE as a tertiary (third) insurance. Recently, when my father went into the hospital, he gave the administrator his insurance card. She looked and him and said, "Wow, you've got enough insurance for three people!" Not quite the case, but it can certainly come in handy, and it's not all that uncommon.

- Robert Hendrick change:healthcare

Primary Insurance

If you are covered by more than one insurance policy, only one can be designated as your primary. That's the one that winds up first in line when your provider goes to collect, and generally the primary insured ends up with the lion's share of the reimbursement responsibility. There may be some guidelines that determine which insurance is primary. If you have Medicare, that's usually the primary. If you have two private insurances, the one you personally hold directly is likely your primary. If you get to elect, consider both policies and their coverage. How much of the premium you are responsible for could also influence your decision. It's hard to predict what the coming year may hold for the health of you and your family, so no matter which insurer you choose, you are assuming part of the risk. If you have a planned event (like pregnancy) or know that there is ongoing treatment, picking the policy that best addresses that particular need can be the wise route to go.

Secondary and Tertiary Insurance

Secondary insurance kicks in after your primary insurance. A provider has to wait to bill a secondary insurance after the primary insurer has processed the claim. If a balance remains outstanding, the provider will then bill the secondary insurance.

Some individuals even have a tertiary insurance, though that is generally limited to those enrolled in Medicare and/or TRICARE supplemental insurances. In that case, the provider must then wait until they receive the EOB from the secondary insurance before billing the tertiary insurance. Because the amount left to be picked up by a tertiary insurance is generally very small, many providers will not bill the tertiary insurance and may require the insured individual to file that claim personally.

All of that complexity makes it a very long process for providers to get paid. That's a big part of why they are so eager to accept a smaller amount in return for prompt payment.

Coordination of Benefits

Determining the amount due and how much each insurance is responsible for when multiple insurers are involved is called **coordination of benefits**. Insurers must agree on who is responsible for which expenses. Some treatments or services may be covered entirely by a primary insurance, or may not. In many instances where Medicare does not provide coverage, a supplemental insurance may.

Taxes and Your Healthcare

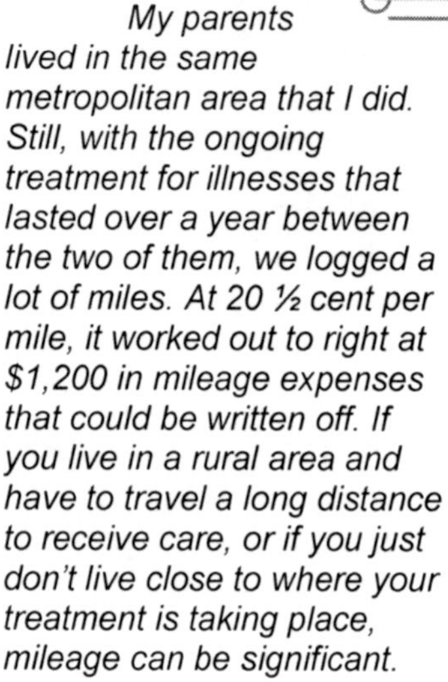

$1,200 in mileage

My parents lived in the same metropolitan area that I did. Still, with the ongoing treatment for illnesses that lasted over a year between the two of them, we logged a lot of miles. At 20 ½ cent per mile, it worked out to right at $1,200 in mileage expenses that could be written off. If you live in a rural area and have to travel a long distance to receive care, or if you just don't live close to where your treatment is taking place, mileage can be significant.

- Christopher Parks
change:healthcare

Medical expenses can stack up. In any given year, 20% of the population accounts for 80% of the medical bills.

If your outlay for medical expenses is more than 7.5% of your **Adjusted Gross Income** (that's the figure for last year's filings from the IRS), then you may be eligible to write off your medical expenses against your taxes. This means you will have to keep track of your expenses and file an itemized report with your return, but the benefit may be worth it.

Many things fall into the category of being tax- deductible. An up-to-date list is available at http://www.irs.gov/publications/p502/index.html on the IRS website.

Some tax deductions are easier to overlook than others. For example, mileage for healthcare purposes can be tax-deductible. So can parking or airline flights. If you've lost your hair due to treatment such as chemotherapy and the doctor prescribes a wig for your well-being, the cost of the wig may be tax deductible. The list changes from time to time, as well as the amount allowed for mileage and the threshold for the write-off. It's best to visit the IRS website and check with an accountant about what is or is not tax-deductible.

What Medical Expenses Are Deductible?

Abortion
Acupuncture
Alcoholism
Ambulance
Artificial Limbs
Artificial Teeth
Autoette
Bandages
Breast Reconstruction Surgery
Birth Control Pills
Braille Books and Magazines
Capital Expenses
Car
Chiropractor
Christian Science Practitioner
Contact Lenses
Crutches
Dental Treatment
Diagnostic Devices
Disabled Dependent Care Expenses
Drug Addiction Treatment
Drugs
Eyeglasses
Eye Surgery
Fertility Enhancement
Founder's Fee
Guide Dog or Other Animal
Health Institute
Health Maintenance Organization
Hearing Aids
Home Care
Home Improvements
Hospital Services
Insurance Premiums
Laboratory Fees
Lead-Based Paint Removal
Learning Disability Education
Legal Fees
Lifetime Care—Advance Pay
Lodging
Long-Term Care
Meals
Medical Conferences
Medical Information Plans
Medical Services
Medicines
Nursing Home
Nursing Services
Operations
Optometrist
Organ Donation Costs
Osteopathy
Oxygen
Prosthesis
Psychiatric Care
Psychoanalysis
Psychologist
Special Education
Special Home for Disabilities
Sterilization
Smoking Cessation Programs
Surgery
Telephone
Television
Therapy
Transplants
Transportation
Trips
Tuition
Vasectomies
Vision Correction Surgery
Weight-Loss Program
Wheelchairs
Wigs
X-rays

What Expenses Are Not Deductible?

Controlled Substances
Cosmetic Surgery
Dancing Lessons
Diaper Service
Electrolysis or Hair Removal
Flexible Spending Account
Funeral Expenses
Future Medical Care
Hair Transplant
Health Club Dues
Health Coverage Tax Credit
Health Savings Accounts
Household Help
Illegal Operations and Treatments
Insurance Premiums
Maternity Clothes
Medical Savings Account (MSA)
Medicines and Drugs from Other Countries
Nonprescription Drugs and Medicines
Nursing Services, Childcare and Babysitting for a Normal, Healthy Baby
Nutritional Supplements
Personal Use Items
Swimming Lessons
Teeth Whitening
Veterinary Fees
Weight-Loss Program (if not medically necessary)

Source: For further clarification and extended information on which items are or are not tax-deductible visit the Internal Revenue Service 2008 publication at http://www.irs.gov/publications/p502/index.html

Other Resources

Best Buy Drugs, from Consumer Reports, provides information to help people choose prescription drugs based on effectiveness, a drug's track record, safety and price. They often de-bunk the "newer is better" myth to recommend drugs that have been on the market longer with a proven track record of safety (which almost always are also cheaper). Check them out at **www.crbestbuydrugs.org**.

PharmMD keeps up with new prescriptions, looks for interactions and helps identify options for reducing medications when a patient has more than they potentially need. Find them at **www.PharmMD.com**

DestinationRX has information on prescriptions including dosages and costs. It can be found at **www.drx.com**

The **IRS website** gives a complete listing of all things that are considered tax-deductible from a medical expense standpoint. That information can be found at **http://www.irs.gov/taxtopics/tc502.html**

FamiliesUSA is a not-for-profit organization dedicated to helping the American healthcare consumer. They have some interesting resources and a very grassroots effort at **www.FamiliesUSA.org**

The website at **www.changehealthcare.com** has information on prescription pricing including price comparisons, a store locator and all the tools you need for managing primary, secondary and tertiary insurances. In addition, the medical billing toolset guides you in determining what medical expenses qualify as tax-deductible based on the IRS guidelines and gives you an itemized report ready to send to your accountant or the IRS with your return.

5

DIRECTING YOUR CARE

Choosing a Provider

So, how do people choose a healthcare provider? We jokingly refer to the factors most people use as the "three C's" – Cost, Conversation and Quality. The truth is that there are a lot of issues that go into that decision, but quality would seem to be what trumps all. But how is "quality" defined?

"Quality" is another of the industry buzz words like transparency. And like transparency, quality is subjective. Ask someone to define quality, and the answer emerges: "I know it when I see it." To the average consumer, selecting a quality provider often comes down to personal preference. Decisions are based on answers to questions like, "Did I like the staff?" and "Was I cured of my illness?" and "Did I receive good treatment?"

What are the elements of quality? Currently there are over 150 quality initiatives taking place, each aimed at helping consumers, employers and insurers identify the elements that make for high quality providers. We speak with people at all income levels, from all walks of life about quality in healthcare. Our conversations are informal, but interesting. Here is some of what we hear.

Outcomes

Generally, the first response we get when we ask someone to define quality is something such as, "It's all about outcomes" – the results. How quickly a patient recovers or even how long they survive is generally most important. There is a significant amount of data that exists on outcomes, but if people are honest with themselves and really dive down into how they've selected a provider, they may realize that documented outcomes received far lower priority in the choice – if it ever was given consideration at all. Oftentimes, it is simply implied based on a provider's reputation.

Some data on outcomes is publicly available. The **Centers for Medicare and Medicaid Services** (CMS) tracks this data for patients with certain conditions. If you want to look at it, you can

Electronic Medical Record (EMR)

The accessibility of your records may be a significant issue for you in selecting a provider. It can have a profound impact on the continuity of care that you receive. An EMR is an Electronic Medical Record. EMRs are used by medical professionals as a means to document and communicate clinical information about patients between providers. An EMR is the new version of that paper manila file folder that seems to magically appear when you go see your doctor. Truth is, each doctor has their own and they don't share well, and that's the real reason for the push to get things electronically. With an EMR the data is portable or able to be accessed by those professionals providing you with care. If you have a medical history (and pretty much everyone does), it helps a physician to know that history when they begin to provide treatment. And it is exclusively the responsibility of the provider to add information.

find it at the CMS website. Be sure you understand what you are looking at. Outcomes should be weighted and easy to read. Hospital outcomes data is available from CMS for consumers at **http://www.hospitalcompare.hhs.gov**

Morbidity rate, or the number of deaths per hundred or thousand with a certain diagnosis, can be a quantifiable metric. Just be sure to take **severity** into account. Severity is the concept that an oncologist specializing in late stage patients is likely to have a higher morbidity rate than an oncologist who sees patients in all stages of cancer.

Provider Experience

This is another available metric, but it is open to interpretation. Experience can be based on either how many years a doctor has been practicing, or how many times a provider performed a certain procedure. Both metrics are readily available for consumers to see at **www.changehealthcare.com** and other sites.

Convenience

In our drive-thru, 24-hour, print-on-demand society, convenience is a major deciding factor. If you've ever been to a retail-based clinic, you know just what we mean. It's usually a heck of a lot shorter wait than the ER or even the doctor's office, but not necessarily of equal or as high quality. You might really like your doc, but if you're really sick, nobody wants to wait until tomorrow.

Convenience may also determine where you get your prescription. Those large chains with a location on virtually every corner are pretty darn convenient. However, that has no

Concierge Services

The ultimate in convenience is concierge services. The model is akin to the old-fashioned notion of doctors making house calls. With a concierge service, patients pay a fee (generally annually) that covers the cost of care by the physician. The physician is expected to make themselves available and even make house calls for these patients. It's not the most cost-effective form of care, but it is becoming increasingly more common.

bearing on whether they fill the order correctly the highest percentage of the time, which could be an important aspect of quality. Furthermore, our research shows that those that are most convenient are often the most expensive.

Location

Having sharp chest pains? I bet you wouldn't drive anywhere other than the closest emergency room. But does your ER perform the most open-heart surgeries? Are they more likely to try a less invasive solution like medication or a stent before cracking open your chest? The three most important things in real estate are location, location and location. That's often true for healthcare.

So how far did you travel for your doc? Did you do a national search to find the best specialists? Did you look internationally? If you live in a small community, you may be fortunate and have a really good set of options for healthcare. But it's doubtful that you have access to the top specialists for your specific need. Chances are, you'd have to travel to a larger city with more than one hospital system to get the better specialists – though there are exceptions. We know of one instance where a top NY specialist decided he wanted the simpler life and

Personal Health Record (PHR)

A PHR is the layman's version of the EMR (Electronic Medical Record). You would use a PHR as a means to keep up with the information that you might normally share with a doctor. It may include information about self-reported glucose levels if you're a diabetic, your mood if you're dealing with depression, your self-recorded blood pressure if you're fighting hypertension, or any number of aspects of your health. Upkeep of PHRs used to be dependent upon the patient. Recently, some PHR models have also started electronically importing information from EMRs for the patient to access.

moved to rural Tennessee (let the theme song from the TV show "Green Acres" play in your head). But that's a "needle in a haystack" as they might say around those parts. Generally speaking, the best specialists are at the hospital systems in major metropolitan cities.

Referral

Location, location and location are the three most important things in real estate, but for providers, it's referral, referral and referral. Most people go to the provider their physician refers them to. Your physicians will direct you to other doctors within their own medical system – probably other physicians associated with the hospital(s) where they may have privileges.

Many of the large hospital systems have an ongoing practice of purchasing outside clinics. While those are viable businesses, and they can justify their purchases through the revenue earned, there is a more important motivation - the referral. Hospitals depend on the front line physicians to make referrals for the higher dollar procedures that their patients will require. The best way for them to ensure they get those referrals is to tie them into the hospital's system.

Narrowing Your Choices

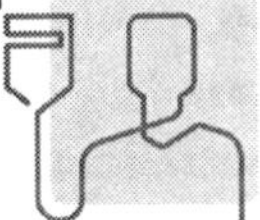

My wife and I have personally gone through a list of doctors within different plans to find out if our family's doctors are listed. That was the deciding factor on which plan we selected. Any future selections were then constrained to some extent, since those providers tend to refer to other providers who are in the same network.

- Robert Hendrick
change:healthcare

Now don't get us wrong; the federally legislated **Stark Amendment**, at the most basic level, prevents doctors from referring patients into businesses from which they profit (however there are many exceptions to the rule, especially in rural areas). But once the doc is part of the hospital's system, the hospital has numerous ways to encourage using its own providers. They may offer administrative and billing services, a common appointment setting system, have ongoing internal communications that let providers know what other services are available and many other incentives. That may all sound trivial, but doctors are busy people, and just like convenience is a factor for you, it is for them, too.

Bedside Manner

How you get along with a physician heavily influences your choice of a provider. It can be the deciding factor in vetoing a doc. Numerous people we talked with have selected doctors because of great reputation, have been referred into them and found them to have all the right experience and credentials. And then, they have rejected those providers because of their bedside manner. Nothing is worse than going to see a provider who rushes you in and out of the office, treating you like "just another patient." It is especially difficult to honestly assess a provider when he or she has been referred to you by someone whom you trust such as your primary care physician.

Cost

Among the well-to-do and very well-insured, we heard, "Cost is not an issue." But don't be fooled

Embracing Technology

Healthcare is stuck in the 80's. The Internet hasn't revolutionized healthcare like it's revolutionized every other industry because the insurance companies are in the way. None of the main players in the industry want transparency. However, consumers sure do want transparency. They also want to connect with their doctors online. That's how everyone communicates nowadays. It's about time your doctor embraces the Internet. It's about time the price you pay for your doctor visit is totally transparent.

- Jay Parkinson, M.D.
Co-Founder Hello Health

by that cavalier attitude! Sure, in situations of life and death, no one asks about the costs. But when it's not, it is all about the dollar. Even if you don't think so, your insurer probably does, and your provider is also trying to watch that dollar as well. Some providers will first try the least invasive and least costly procedures before moving into more expensive procedures and/or referring you to a specialist. It may be in part because that's what the insurer will allow, and it may be an effort by your provider to try to keep the expenses down because they are often allowed a fixed amount to treat a condition. So even if cost is not an issue, be aware that it is distinctly a factor in your care and may be part of the determination of when and to which specialist(s) you ultimately get referred.

There are other issues regarding cost. Some providers are better than others at knowing what services must be **pre-authorized**, and what is or is not covered by your insurer. Bear in mind that those are different from one insurance policy to the next, and that those are factors that could determine what part of the bill you get stuck with at the end of the day. Providers who are on top of their pre-authorization and determination of what is covered may do a good job of making sure they get the insurer to pay most of the bill and minimize the cost to their patients. If they are not, you may wind up with more of the bill than you would have had with another provider who did a better job. Therefore, it's important to see how your provider fares in what the patient is left paying versus other providers of the same services and procedures.

Cost can be a major consideration for the uninsured, the underinsured and those receiving treatment outside of their network. The rates that providers bill, get reimbursed – receive payment through insurance and their patients – are all readily available at many consumer website which promote transparency. Check out your provider on the change:healthcare website.

Network

Your insurance network plays a strong role in determining your providers. This is a factor that relates closely to cost, since going out-of-network generally could imply a higher cost to you for a provider's services. Once you are in a network, there is an incentive to stay in-network because the cost of going out-of-network is potentially much higher in terms of what you will be asked to pay out-of-pocket.

Your insurer will provide you with a directory of providers who are in-network. What about those who are not? You'll have to go someplace else for that list. The change:healthcare website provides you with a nationwide list of physicians, hospitals and pharmacies independent of the list of whom your insurance company may have in their network.

Patients As Consumers

Healthcare consumerism has introduced new relationships into the American healthcare system. The days of the passive patient blindly following the wisdom of the demi-god doctor are gone. This is a new day of shared medical decision-making, wherein consumers partner with their providers to make decisions regarding achieving the best healthcare value (outcomes/price). The new math of healthcare value demands that in addition to pricing transparency (cost), that other outcome metrics like convenient access and high quality (in both service rendered as well as the service experience) will play an equally important role in the transition to next generation healthcare.

- Scott Shreeve, M.D.

The Water Cooler and Over the Fence

Choosing your healthcare provider is arguably the most important healthcare decision you will make. It can literally be a life-and-death decision. And what ultimately decides where you go comes down to that conversation that you have over the back fence with your neighbor, over the water cooler conversation with a co-worker (who, by the way, shares the same network you do through your common employer), or over coffee with a friend.

If your source is a qualified medical professional, that opinion carries great weight. But if it's not, it's really only an assessment of that person's personal experience. Then the person is relating his personal outcome, the convenience of the doctor, the distance he traveled, the referral given to him from another physician, the amount the insurer did not cover, the doctor's bedside manner, his compatibility with that physician's personality or the conversation that he had with someone else over the fence or at the water cooler. You can't always rely on these sources for accurate recommendations.

What's a Responsible Healthcare Consumer to Do?

Do your research. Seek out the quantifiable data and select a few providers. Call around. Ask about them. Google™ them. See what other people are saying about them. And when all else fails, go see them. Make an office visit. See what you think. After all, it's your health we're talking about here, not that annoying guy in accounting.

Medical Billing Errors

According to *MONEY Magazine*, more than 90% of hospital bills contain errors![6] Wow! That's a failing grade by ANY standard. But finding those errors can be tough. Some things are easier to catch than others. Some you have to cut through the medical jargon to even begin to understand the bill.

Medical coders are the people who ultimately are responsible for the makeup of a medical bill. They key in services and products provided based on the records kept by the providers. Coders are responsible for reviewing records and recording whether a bypass was a single, double or triple and billing accordingly. But they were not present when care was rendered, so they rely on the records produced by the provider to

[6] Dolan, Daria and Ken Dolan. "With Billing Errors Rampant, You Need Our Tips on How Not to Overpay for Medical Care." *MONEY Magazine* Oct. 1995. June 11, 2008 <http://money.cnn.com/magazines/moneymag/moneymag_archive/1995/10/01/206600/index.htm>

determine what should be billed. It's a system fraught with unintentional errors.

A great example of how the pharmacy process can generate errors can be found in this *USA Today* article online at **http://tinyurl.com/257htv**

Here's what you can do to try and catch those errors:

- Keep a record of tests performed by a provider
- Keep a record of services and medications provided
- Ask questions of providers and the office staff when you don't understand

There are even consultants called "patient advocates" who understand coding and billing. For a fee, they offer services to review your medical bills and negotiate with providers on your behalf. It can be time consuming, but their intimate knowledge of the healthcare system gives them a distinct advantage in negotiating. In fact, you may be able to accomplish the same or comparable results simply by picking up the phone and spending some time haggling for a lower rate with the person on the other end of the line. But when you simply cannot cut through the obscure language, a patient advocate may be able to help.

MedSpeak and InsuranceSpeak

Medical billing is done in terms of codes – **ICD, DRG** and **CPT** codes, to be exact. Each code has a unique purpose and the codes are complex. Certified coders must be trained and many have attained advanced degrees to reach true proficiency. Breaking through the coding is not just a chapter, but a book unto itself. We've provided a basic clarification of the codes so that you can at least be aware of the jargon that runs throughout the industry.

ICD codes or International Classification of Diseases codes are primarily used by hospitals and doctors to identify and classify health issues and hospital procedures. There is a numeric identifier and a description for each issue and procedure. That description can often be arcane and bear little if any similarity to more common lay terms. For example, an open-heart bypass surgery might be referred to as a CABG or Coronary Artery Bypass Graft. There are 28 possible ICD procedure codes that can be used to convey this health issue, such as; code 36.01 "Open chest coronary artery angioplasty" or code 36.07 "Insertion of drug-eluting coronary artery stent(s)". There are thousands of ICD codes that can be used to classify a diagnosis. More importantly to doctors and hospitals, the diagnosis ultimately determines the reimbursement amount to the provider.

DRG or **Diagnosis Related Groups** codes are used by hospitals to group an **inpatient** admission's ICD codes primarily for submitting reimbursement claims to Medicare and other insurances. The DRGs work by grouping the 10,000+ ICD codes into a more manageable number of patient categories, close to 500 now. Patients treated within each category share similar health issues and utilize similar services.

As with ICD coding, there is a numeric identifier and a description for each DRG. Following our previous CABG example, ICD codes for a CABG procedure performed in the hospital most likely would be

Mistakes Happen

My father was in the final stages of his life and had been retired for several years. However, someone miscoded the bill for his ventilator as worker's compensation, and as a result the claim was denied. I called up the insurer and told them if they could explain to me how a seventy-five year old man on a ventilator for the last several months could possibly be working a part-time job simultaneously, I would gladly pay the bill. They promptly reviewed the claim and approved the coverage. Mistakes happen all of the time with medical bills. Check yours for anything that seems inconsistent.

- Christopher Parks
change:healthcare

grouped under DRG 548 "Percutaneous Cardiovascular Procedures with AMI without CC" (AMI means Acute Myocardial Infraction; CC stands for Complications and Co-morbidities). Simple, huh?

CPT or **Current Procedural Codes** are numeric codes used primarily by physicians and outpatient clinics to identify medical, surgical and diagnostic services performed. These codes are then used to communicate the services delivered with the insurer, when filing a claim for the purpose of reimbursement. CPT has a similar level of complexity.

If it all sounds like Greek (actually it's probably closer to Latin, but that's little consolation), don't be intimidated. Many hospitals have patient advocates on staff who can help you understand the codes. But remember who pays their salary. If you think you have an issue, you might do well to seek out a patient advocate who works just for you. Check the resources at the end of the chapter for some patient advocates who offer services to both individuals and to large employers.

Denial of Coverage

When an insurer will not approve and/or pay for a treatment or service, it's called **denial of service** (also known as **denial of coverage** or **denial of claim**), and it can be for any number of reasons.

Treatments are approved for certain diagnoses. Others are not. So for example, if there is a patient with a blocked artery, open-heart surgery may be an approved procedure for correcting the problem. However, if the diagnosis is coded incorrectly and the patient is given a diagnosis code for pneumonia, the surgery likely will be denied as not being an approved treatment for the inaccurately recorded pneumonia.

When there is a denial of coverage, or when a bill just doesn't add up, the dispute resolution process can be complicated. Not only will you need to call the provider, but you will also need to call your insurance company. If you are uninsured, it can be even more difficult to know exactly what services you received or to work with the provider to get your bill corrected. If there is a dispute to resolve, it can be in your best interest to consider retaining a patient advocate to help you through the denial of claim issue. At the very least, you should ask for clarification in writing from your insurer as to exactly why the claim was denied.

Maximum Lifetime Benefit

If you are unfortunate enough to have a catastrophic health event, it is possible to reach the limit on what your insurance will pay out. That amount is referred to as the maximum lifetime benefit. Generally, this is tied to a specific insurance, and since most insurance relationships last only 2-3 years, the maximum lifetime benefit is not commonly reached. However, a catastrophic event with an extended hospital stay, long-term therapy and/or long-term care can quickly push an individual to that limit.

Pre-existing Conditions

A pre-existing condition is a health condition, injury or sickness that you have already been diagnosed with or received treatment for prior to enrollment in a new health plan. Depending on the new health insurance plan, the participant may be subject to a waiting period before they can receive care for that condition. Often if the participant does not disclose their pre-existing conditions, any treatment for that condition or injury could be denied coverage indefinitely.

Some of the more common reasons claims may be legitimately denied are:

- You have hit your maximum lifetime benefit
- You have a non-covered or experimental treatment (this happens with some cancer treatments)
- You have a pre-existing condition that is still outside of coverage

- You experience a lapse in coverage and a health event manifests during that period of time when you did not have coverage

Lapse in Coverage

When a person is between insurances and without coverage, that is called having a "lapse in coverage." Oftentimes when a lapse occurs, it is due to the cost of the policy, and the policy is dropped as a short-term cost-savings measure. However, whether it is a health issue that prompts a person to resume coverage or simply a change in the financial disposition of that person, it is common that insurers will point to that lapse as the point in time at which an ailment manifested itself. Whether that is true or not, it is often a very effective means for an insurer to deny coverage.

Remember that most states allow insurers to cancel policies after patients rack up large medical bills if the insurer finds out the applicant purposefully – or in some states, even accidentally – left out medical details in the application. Insurers claim that ability to revoke policies is needed to protect them against fraud. You be the judge on that one.

Cost-Saving Options

There are many different ways to save on healthcare costs other than simple negotiation after the fact. Not all are applicable in each situation, and you have to use your own best judgment on when cost-saving is an important factor to consider in your care.

Retail-Based Clinics

Many metropolitan areas are seeing the introduction of the **Retail-Based Clinic (RBC)**. These are urgent care centers usually co-located with a pharmacy, department store or grocery store. RBCs provide non-emergency care. Their services are generally provided on demand, often making them more accessible than an ER or even a primary care physician.

For more common ailments, these providers offer convenience and generally lower costs than traditional providers. These facilities are usually staffed by an on-site Registered Nurse (RN) or Nurse Practitioner rather than a fully-credentialed M.D. There is, however, operational and medical supervision by a nearby physician, just not one who is immediately on the premises. By eliminating the need for the traditional office staff (receptionist, nurses, back office staff, etc.), they are able to offer services at a savings to the consumer. However, an RBC is not a substitute to a primary care physician or specialist. RBCs will refer more severe cases to qualified professionals, and will in some cases deny care to high-risk patients (i.e. patients with chronic conditions such as Multiple Sclerosis, cancer, diabetes, etc.).

Other Resources

Dr. Jay Parkinson is a physician who runs a concierge service in New York City and is a founder of Hello Health. His business model is an industry leader in how medical concierge services are rendered. Dr. Parkinson can be found at **www.JayParkinsonMD.com**

OrganizedWisdom Health is the first human-powered, doctor-guided search service for health. The site provides hand-crafted search result pages called WisdomCards™, for the most popular health search terms and phrases without the clutter, redundant links or index spam typically found in search engines. Check them out at **http://organizedwisdom.com**

ReliefInSite is a secure web service that enables pain sufferers to track their conditions. It functions like a diary and organizes patient entries into reports that can be shared online with providers, family members and friends. It can be found at **www.reliefinsite.com**

HealthGrades provides its proprietary quality ratings for physicians and hospitals at **www.healthgrades.com**

Zagat (yes, the same people who rate restaurants and hotels) recently announced their initiative to begin providing quality ratings for the healthcare industry through a partnership with WellPoint. This new online survey tool is hosted by WellPoint and available to their insurance members through their website.

PatientsLikeMe has communities specifically for ALS, ACS and MS. New communities for HIV/AIDS, depression, Parkinson's Disease and others are expanding daily. PatientsLikeMe provides a comprehensive tool for patients with these diseases to document everything from their medications to their mood and physical condition. It can be found at **www.PatientsLikeMe.com**

PATIENT ADVOCATE AND TERMINOLOGY RESOURCES

Medical Bill Review Services Inc. works primarily with individuals and companies to help people with a significant number of medical claims. They charge a flat annual fee and can be found at **www.MedBillReview.com**

Health Advocate works primarily with large employers to help their employees better manage their healthcare. They not only help negotiate with providers and insurers, but also provide auditing services to identify billing errors and help recover costs that should not have been paid. They can be found at **www.healthadvocate.com**

GorillaBill offers tools, resources and services to help you manage the financial side of your health. They provide a Better Health Toolkit, Medical Bill Translator and other great services. Log on to **www.GorillaBill.com** to find out more.

RETAIL-BASED CLINICS

Minute Clinic is the CVS chain of in-store, retail-based clinics. They provide non-acute care and services such as strep throat tests. They can be found online at **www.MinuteClinic.com**

There are a multitude of retail-based clinics and more appear every day. To find more information and a list of clinics go to **www.convenientcareassociation.org/cliniclocations.htm** for a complete look.

The website at **www.changehealthcare.com** has all the tools you need for managing your medical bills, payments and EOBs as well as information on reimbursement rates for Medicare and private insurance.

6

SELECTING THE RIGHT PATH

Choosing a Plan – The Whack-A-Mole Game

There are always trade-offs when it comes to health insurance plans. If you save on one aspect, you stand to lose on

Individual, Couple or Family Plan

If you are single, the individual plan is the only option. That's the easy choice. For couples and families, it's not so simple. Oftentimes, couples will have competing plans offered through each employer. Plans can be difficult to compare and the costs may vary depending on how the group is rated, what coverages are provided and what portion of the premium the employer has their employees pick up. It's best to sit down and compare the plans side-by-side and coverage-for-coverage to see which option offers you the best alternatives.

It is often possible to have coverage through both spouses or for one to carry family coverage and the other to carry an individual policy. Check with your employer to be sure that you get the best mix for your particular situation.

another. Healthcare is truly a high dollar game, and it's your well-being at stake.

There's a popular arcade game with a half-dozen holes and a foam rubber covered mallet. You hit moles with the mallet when they pop up out of the holes. If you hit one mole, another one pops up someplace else. Hit that one and another one pops up. Hit that one and the first one might pop up again.

That's health insurance.

Lower premiums equal less coverage and/or more limited choice of providers. More coverage equals higher premiums and/or more choice of providers. Maybe you take an 80/20 plan to lower your monthly premium, but a single major medical event with a $100,000 bill could cost you $20,000 or more. Hit the mole again.

The challenge for healthcare consumers is to understand their personal health as completely as possible, predict what their healthcare needs will be for the coming year and select the best plan accordingly. But significant medical events are not so easy to predict. You can't plan for torn ligaments, or you may be unaware that you are genetically predisposed to a medical condition.

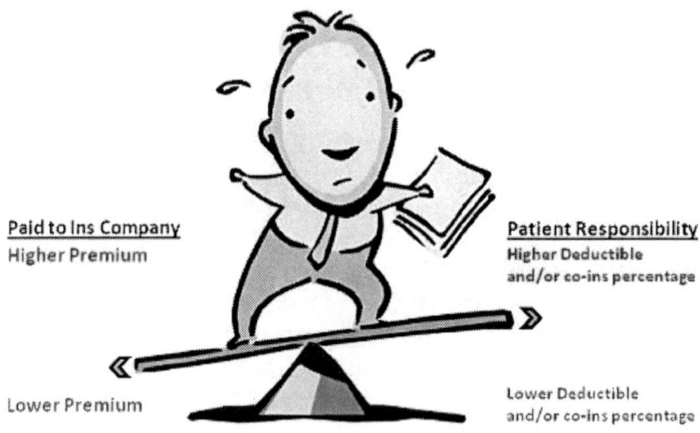

Typically, the 80/20 plan is going to have a less costly premium than the 90/10 plan because the insurer is on the hook for less. The 100% plan is going to be the most costly premium. 100% co-insurance is more commonly seen now with high-deductible health plans, where consumers can be responsible for as much as $5000 of their initial costs. As the deductible goes up, the cost goes down because you are responsible for more in a major medical situation.

HMO, PPO, FSA and HSA Tradeoffs

If it's benefits enrollment time and you have more than one plan from which to select, you need to make an educated decision. Watch for the trade-offs between each plan and see where you think you have the best fit. Most people don't plan on a major medical event, but it's always best to be sure you'll have it covered if you do. The checklist at the end of this chapter will help you to assess which plan may be best for you.

Virtually all plans are either an HMO or a PPO. Other plan types are simply HMO/PPO variations that send you right back into a whack-a-mole game.

Vision

Vision coverage applies to glasses and other basic eye care. Benefits are generally limited to an annual stipend for glasses and/or contact lenses as well as the associated annual checkup. More in-depth services such as taking care of cataracts, amblyopia and other serious eye-related health conditions may be covered under the general healthcare policy.

HMO

A **Healthcare Management Organization** or **HMO** is a type of **Managed Care Organization** (MCO) that provides a form of health insurance coverage that is fulfilled through hospitals, doctors and other providers with which the HMO has a contract. Those are called **participating providers** or are said to be in-network. Under this model, providers form a contract with an HMO to receive more patients, and in return usually agree to provide services at a discount. This option is both cost- and health-driven.

In addition to using their contracts with providers to secure services at a lower price, HMOs hope to gain an advantage over traditional insurance plans by managing their patients' healthcare and reducing unnecessary services. To achieve this, most HMOs require members to select a **primary care physician** (PCP), a doctor who acts as a "**gatekeeper**" for medical services. PCPs are usually internists, pediatricians, family doctors or general practitioners. In a typical HMO, most medical request must first go through the PCP, who authorizes referrals to specialists or other doctors if deemed necessary. Emergency medical care does not require prior authorization from a PCP, and many plans allow women to select an Obstetrician/Gynecologist, whom they may see without a referral, in addition to a PCP. In some cases, chronically ill

Dental

Dental coverage is increasingly rare. It is one of the benefits of healthcare coverage which has been largely eliminated from health plans. Many dentists will not accept insurance, or will not file the claim. They will require that their patients make payment at the time of service, and then let the patients file the claim themselves for reimbursement. The benefits under dental are often limited to basic preventative care (i.e. cleanings and x-rays). For that reason, the coverage is generally priced at the actual cost of the benefit plus an administrative charge, and is not considered very cost-effective. Also, as a result, the rates for dental services can vary widely since coverage is sparse and insurers cannot effectively negotiate rates.

patients may be allowed to select a specialist in the field of their illness as a PCP.

HMOs often provide preventive care for a lower co-payment, or even for free, in order to keep members from developing an avoidable condition that would require a great deal of medical services. This inclusion of services intended to maintain a member's health gave the HMO its name. Some services, such as outpatient mental health care, are often provided on a limited basis. More costly forms of care, diagnosis or treatment may not be covered at all.

Behavioral (Mental) Health

Behavioral or Mental Health coverage usually falls under its own heading. Behavioral health benefits are typically capped at a few thousand dollars ($10,000 or less annually) when offered. For that reason, many behavioral health facilities are self-pay. Add to that the stigma often associated (and unjustly so) with behavioral health, and many people will opt to self-pay out of their own pocket to avoid the risk that their employer or co-workers will be made aware of their condition.

PPO

A **Preferred Provider Organization** or **PPO** is a managed care organization of medical doctors, hospitals and other health care providers who have contracted with an insurer or a third-party administrator to provide health care at reduced rates to the insurer's or administrator's clients. This option is primarily chosen due to financial benefits.

PPO and HMO's Lesser Known Cousin: POS

POS refers to Point-of-Service plans. Much like with a HMO, in a POS plan you must select a primary care physician who will direct your referral within the POS network. You will also have little to no deductible and pay a small co-payment up front. Similar to a PPO, if you choose to see a provider who is out-of-network, you are likely to be subject to a deductible and your co-payment will become 30-40% of the provider's total charges.

The idea of using a PPO is that the providers will provide the insured members of the group a substantial discount below their regularly-charged rates. This will be mutually beneficial in theory, as the insurer will be billed at a reduced rate when its policy holders utilize the services of the "preferred" provider, and the provider will see an increase in its business because almost all insurance recipients in the organization will use only providers who join the organization or network. PPOs negotiate with providers in order to set fee schedules and handle disputes between insurers and providers. PPOs can also contract with one another to strengthen their positions in certain geographic areas without having to form new relationships directly with providers.

PPOs differ from health maintenance organizations (HMOs) in that those insured under an HMO who do not use participating healthcare providers receive little or no benefit from their health plan. PPO members will be reimbursed for utilization of non-preferred providers, albeit at a reduced rate which may include higher deductibles, co-payments, lower reimbursement percentages or any combination of the above.

Finding, Selecting and Providing Coverage

As a small business owner, deciding which (if any) health insurance to get was THE biggest pain since opening our doors. Before we had any employees, I was denied coverage by one company due to elevated cholesterol levels. It was incredibly frightening thinking I would have no way to pay for care for my family in the event of an emergency. Luckily, we had someone in our extended family who knew the twists and turns of the industry, and was able to help us find a company and a plan that worked for us. If it had not been for the "translator" in the family, we may not have had the right coverage in place, and may have been denied certain procedures due to cost - the same procedures the doctors needed to save our son's life.

-Chris Blanz
Cabedge

Consumer Directed Health Plans (CDHP)

The rules for healthcare changed dramatically with the introduction of Consumer Directed Healthcare Plans (CDHP). These include the Healthcare Savings Account (HSA) and Healthcare Reimbursement Account (HRA). The Flexible Spending Account (FSA) serves more as stepping stone into a true CDHP. High-deductible health plans with HSAs and HRAs

Health Insurance State-by-State

Health insurance is regulated on a state-by-state basis. Each insurer has to be licensed in each state they are in or else have an agreement with an insurer in another state to offer coverage there.

There are a handful of large insurers who operate in most (if not all) states, and many more medium and small-sized insurers. Here are some of the national players:

- Wellpoint™
- Aetna®
- Blue Cross/Blue Shield
- Cigna
- Humana®
- United Healthcare® / Golden Rule®

The Blues: Blue Cross/Blue Shield

Blue Cross/Blue Shield is the single largest private healthcare insurer in the U.S. They are unique in that they are a collection of 39 franchises with regional exclusivity – their geographic coverage areas do not overlap, and they offer some sort of coverage in all 50 states. Some of "The Blues" are for profit. Some are not. Some cover more than one state. Others not.

As a result, there are variations from one franchise to the next; just look at their EOBs for a start – no two are exactly alike.

But as a group, they were one of the first big health insurers. And they enjoy the advantage of a pretty big slice of the pie in some places – a 65% market share in the state of Tennessee for example. That gives them a lot of clout with providers and a lot of leverage when negotiating rates.

are fairly new to the industry and continue to gain traction as healthcare costs rise. At the most basic level, CDHPs shift initial costs down to the individual or family utilizing the health plan by setting a high deductible. The minimum individual deductible to quality for a CDHP is around $1,100 and family about $2,200. This high deductible helps to reduce premiums and engage the plan participants in the cost of their healthcare, by asking them to spend money both themselves and their employer has contributed to the HSA or HRA.

Health Savings Accounts (HSA)

Under an HSA plan, you have a savings account from which medical expenses are paid until you reach your deductible. The concept of a co-pay is largely gone. You pay the whole portion – the portion that used to be what you and your insurance company paid together. You should still get the benefit of the negotiated allowed rate so long as you stay in-network. But you pay now what had once been the insurance company's responsibility as well.

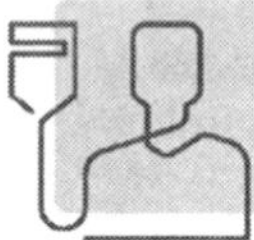

Even Doctors Are Learning

The doctors managing my daughter's Crohn's disease know that we are on a high deductible health plan. They have worked with us to balance her medications and to give us samples of new medications to try before writing us a prescription. That way, we are not draining funds from our HSA. Doctors are becoming more attuned to high deductible plans and working with their patients to help them maintain their health and their costs.

- Nashville Healthcare CEO

Once you've met the deductible amount, your insurance should kick in and provide full coverage according to your plan depending on whether it's a 100%, 90/10 or 80/20.

If you fund the account, that money is yours. Unlike in an FSA (see the next section), the HSA money does not evaporate at the end of the policy period. It is earmarked for medically-related expenses, but you have control of it. If you move to a new insurance policy or even a new employer, you get to keep the account. The only limitation is that it remains for the express purpose of medical expenses.

An HSA is used in conjunction with a PPO network. If you have a good health history and no major medical conditions, this can be an ideal plan. It allows you to set aside and save money, and if your employer is going to generously contribute to the plan, it holds costs down for both you and your employer. The downside is that these plans usually also feature high deductibles.

With an HSA, you need to be comfortable with making your healthcare purchasing decisions. Be sure that the plan has tools to help you do cost comparisons, and review those tools before making the decision to go with an HSA.

If you have multiple insurances (lucky you!) through a spouse or otherwise, the HSA may **not** be right for you. Many HSA plans do not allow secondary insurances.

Flexible Spending Account (FSA)

An FSA is a "use it or lose it" plan. Under an FSA, your employer funds an account for you for medical needs, although it can also be used for a lot of other purposes such as daycare expenditures. You can also contribute your own money to the account with pre-tax dollars. If you use the funds in that account during any given year, it is withdrawn from the account. If you don't, then your employer pulls the money back at the end of each year. It may seem a bit unfair, but it provides an incentive to your employer to encourage you to be healthy and support your health by providing wellness programs like weight control programs, flu shots, etc. If you anticipate having a significant amount of medical expenses, this may be a good plan for you. If you're relatively healthy and don't foresee a need for as much healthcare, this may not be the best plan.

Disease Management

Employer-sponsored programs that encourage better health practices among their employees and family in order to decrease healthcare costs are called **disease management** programs. Increasingly, companies are finding support among insurers and in legal decisions that endorse putting more responsibility for an insured's health on the individual. More employers are offering incentives in the form of premium reimbursements to employees who meet certain criteria such as weight or body mass index (BMI) thresholds, actively manage and document their handling of chronic diseases like diabetes and/or don't smoke.

There are even occasional cases where employers provide healthcare coverage, but have managed to legally exclude employees who smoke or use tobacco products. Individuals are increasingly being held responsible for the lifestyle choices they have made as it relates to the cost of their health and well-being. Be aware of your employer's policies, and how they might impact your coverage.

Why Do Premiums Vary?

Different premium prices are somewhat easily explained. Different insurers get different rates with providers. Some insurers have better leverage than others do in certain areas, usually because they are well-entrenched and have built up a large group of insured people. Some plans include providers who get reimbursed at a higher rate.

If you are insured through your employer or your spouse, the company providing the insurance is rated as a group. Most insurers conduct a census of ALL employees. They want to know what the pool of people is like so that they can assess their risk. They get information on everyone because they never know when someone new may decide to pick up coverage. People's life situations change. Change in marital status, a change in a spouse's job situation or other outside factors can cause an employee to decide to pick up or drop coverage without much prior notice.

The size of the covered group can play a big role in the cost of health insurance. The bigger the group, the easier it is to assess, and the more people over whom risk can be spread; so oftentimes, the lower the rate. The smaller the group, the less predictable it is, and therefore the higher the rate. However, a larger company with an older workforce may see higher rates since frequency and severity of health issues tend to increase with age.

Insurers prefer predictability. Remember, they are similar to the Las Vegas bookmakers – they are playing the odds. Larger groups are far more predictable than small ones. Therefore, insurers must compensate for the unpredictable nature of smaller groups by charging a higher rate.

The Single Most Important Question

If you only get one question right on the insurance application, it's the one where they ask if you have existing coverage or not. Get that one wrong and you are in for years of undue stress and potential financial burden. A lapse in coverage is the single easiest means for an insurer to deny coverage by simply implying that a condition originated during that period in which a person lacked healthcare insurance. So when asked if you have existing coverage, if you are giving up existing coverage for the new, answer that you ***do*** *have coverage.*

- Chris Hartnett
Rousell & Associates

Individual vs. Group Policies

As discussed in the section above, insurance companies are all about assessing and managing risk. That's why individual insurance policies can cost more than similar plans associated with a group. Imagine a fleet of ships carrying the Queen's loot from England to America. Her prized possessions are much safer and likely to reach shore if they are distributed and carried amongst 9 ships rather than 1. It's the same line of thinking. On an individual policy, any health issues or previous claims loom large on the radar of the insurer as risk. Consider a 4-person family looking to get coverage directly from the insurance company. One person with a serious health issue is a 25% chance of hitting the insurer big. For a 100-person employer, 25% of the group having major health issues is less likely.

Getting a policy as an individual or as a family, without the help of an employer, can be incredibly difficult – and expensive. Luckily, the federal government requires insurers to sell policies to people who lose group coverage – including those laid off from their jobs. This is referred to as COBRA – the Consolidated Omnibus Budget Reconciliation Act – which allows individuals to extend their group health benefits. The group health plan can be extended for a limited amount of time under several different circumstances including voluntary or involuntary job loss, reduction in hours, transition between jobs or divorce. Details may vary state to state.

Self-Funded Employers

Large employers are allowed to create their own "pool" and be self-funded. Companies with as few as 25 employees may do this. The companies hire the insurance industry odds makers – or actuaries – who predict the amount of money the employer will need to hold in reserve to pay for claims. However, if the employer is not in the business of healthcare it will be poorly equipped to deal with administering a healthcare plan. There are

Is Your Employer Self-Funded?

It's not so easy to tell. You might have a large insurance company's card in your wallet or purse, but that doesn't mean it is your insurer. It may just be the network your company's TPA uses. Self-funded companies generally contract with a TPA or insurance company to administer their healthcare, and companies with as few as 25 employees may be self-funded.

rates to be negotiated, payments to be made to providers, claims to be reviewed and more. So, they get help.

Self-funded employers contract with a **TPA** or **Third Party Administrator** to handle the claims. The TPA can be an insurance company. So, while it may appear that your insurance is from a large insurance company with a name that you recognize, they may just be doing the hard work for your employer.

Making a Choice

Remember - always do your homework when comparing plans, whether you are purchasing an individual policy or selecting a plan through your employer. Assess your expected situation for the coming year and select accordingly. Here are a few things to pay attention to when selecting a health plan.

Before you choose a plan:

- Look to see what kind of organization you are dealing with. **Is it a HMO, PPO or POS plan?** At the most basic level, this will determine how you manage your provider relationships over the next year. HMOs are typically more restrictive and require referrals, but they generally have low out-of-pocket costs. PPOs are generally less restrictive when it comes to provider selection, however they typically have higher initial out-of-pocket costs. POS plans, on the other hand, provide the largest amount of provider selection, yet they typically mean higher costs when you choose to go out-of-network.
- **Look at the plan options** and decide what is most important to you. Is it your yearly out-of pocket cost? Your deducible and premium amounts?
- Next look at the **network**. Do you have a wide selection of providers? And always double-check to see if your most important providers are in-network. For example, you may decide it is important to have your children's pediatrician in-network.

- See **how the pharmacy plans compare**. Some will have a standard co-payment on brand name drugs, while other plans have lower co-payments on "preferred" brand name drugs or generics.
- Double-check to see **which local and regional hospitals are in-network** (if you have multiple options).
- Always read over the **dental, vision, and behavioral health coverage** within the policy if there is no supplemental coverage being offered. There are often limits on this kind of healthcare.
- Finally, remember **there is always a trade-off!!**

Once you select your plan:

- Make sure to **disclose your pre-existing conditions** during enrollment. This is especially important for PPOs, which commonly have waiting periods. You are always better to be subjected to a waiting period for care, than be denied coverage later because you did not disclose your current medical condition(s).
- **Read your policy**! Be aware of the benefits you are being provided and how to use them. Call and ask questions – especially if you are unsure if a provider is in-network.
- Know and understand your **appeals process**.

There will always be factors outside of your control, so be sure to plan as best you can. If you opt for the plan with the high deductible, make sure to put aside enough to cover the expense in case you need to do so. If you are expecting a child, you may want to include family coverage. If your spouse is unsure of a job situation, you may want to elect to purchase spousal coverage through your employer. Plan accordingly.

Other Resources

Healthways is one of the leading disease/wellness program providers in the country. They market primarily to employers, but have consumer tools like information on smoking cessation programs and weight loss programs available at **www.healthways.com**

Vimo provides information and comparisons for individuals looking to secure healthcare coverage. They can be found at **www.vimo.com**

Your broker can be a great source of information on your specific plan. Ask the insurance agent who provides your insurance when you have specific questions about your coverage.

The **change:healthcare** website has all the tools you need for managing your medical bills, payments and EOBs as well as information on reimbursement rates for Medicare and private insurance. A relatively complete listing of health insurers can be found at **www.changehealthcare.com**.

The National Association of Health Underwriters, website **www.nahu.org** has a section for consumers which contains the Healthy Access Database and consumer guides. These guides are comprehensive and provide information on a wide range of topics from individual health insurance to long-term care. Check them out at **www.nahu.org/consumer/healthcare/index.cfm**.

The **Henry J. Kaiser Family Foundation** has multiple websites that provide free up-to-date health information and data. **Statehealthfacts.org** provides data for all 50 states, as well as information on more than 500 health topics.

7

Medicare, Medicaid and TRICARE

Medicare

Medicare covers 44 million Americans who are eligible as retirees. If you are part of the **sandwich generation**, those of us with our children's healthcare to attend to as well as that of our elderly parents, you may need to be familiar with the basics of **Medicaid, Medicare** and **TRICARE**. There are many intricacies in dealing with Medicare from which plans to select to when you enroll. Navigating Medicare is a book in and of itself. However, as it relates to understanding and interacting with your benefits, Medicare works in much the same way as private insurance. There are still bills, statements, EOBs and payments.

The History of Medicare

The idea for a national healthcare system originally began with President Truman in 1945. About twenty years later, Medicare was signed into law by president Lyndon B. Johnson. Today Medicare is the largest single payor of healthcare expenses in the United States. This national health insurance program, created and administered by the federal government, is designed to address the medical needs of older American citizens.

Medicare is available to U.S. citizens 65 years of age and older and some people under age 65 who have a disability, such as those with end-stage renal disease, debilitating stroke, etc.

Medicare is financed through Social Security contributions, monthly premiums paid by program participants and general government revenues. Medicare is funded solely by the federal government. States do NOT make matching contributions to the Medicare fund.

Insurance coverage provided by Medicare is similar to that offered by private health insurance carriers. Medicare usually pays 50–80% of the medical bill, while the patient pays the remaining balance for services provided. Because there are costs not covered, ranging anywhere from 20-50% of the bill, Medicare recipients often pick up a secondary insurance to help cover the remaining balance.

Mark Your Calendar!
Medicare Open Enrollment

Medicare Open Enrollment takes place in ***November*** of each year when the government opens up its rolls to admit new enrollees.

Medicare coverage is defined by the various categories of care provided:

Medicare Part A provides basic coverage for hospital stays and post-hospital nursing facilities, home health care and hospice care for patients. Most people automatically receive Part A when they turn 65 and do not have to pay a premium because they and/or their spouse paid Medicare taxes while they were working.

Medicare Part B covers most fees associated with basic doctor visits and laboratory testing. It also pays for some outpatient medical services such as medical equipment, supplies, home health care and physical therapy. However, these services and supplies are only covered by Part B when medically necessary and prescribed by a doctor. Enrollment in Part B is optional for people ages 65 and older and Medicare recipients pay a small premium per month for these added benefits. The amount of the premium is periodically adjusted. Not every person who receives Medicare Part A enrolls in Part B.

The Medicare Donut Hole

In the world of Medicare, the **Donut Hole** is not a tasty little morsel, it's a rude little surprise for many Medicare Part D enrollees. The term refers to a portion of prescription costs that Medicare enrollees are expected to pick up. In 2008, the gap began after $2,510 in annual prescription costs had been paid by Medicare. The next $2,500 or more in prescription costs for the calendar year fell to the enrollee before Medicare picked back up under catastrophic care. This can lead to rationing or skipping prescriptions. According to an August 2005 study conducted by USAToday, Kaiser Family Foundation and Harvard School of Public Health, nearly 29% of people have skipped or rationed a prescription because they were unable to afford the cost of the prescription.

Medicare Part C

permits Medicare recipients to select coverage from among various private healthcare plans to include HMOs, PPOs, POS plans, **Medical Savings Accounts** (MSA), **fee-for-service plans** and **provider-sponsored plans**. These plans will receive a per capita payment per enrollee from the federal government, and the plans have the option to charge the enrollees a monthly premium. Individuals who are eligible for Medicare Part A and are enrolled in Medicare Part B are eligible for enrollment in either the traditional Medicare program or this new Medicare Part C program. Each November, the health care financing administration conducts open enrollment periods so that people may select the type of health care program in which they wish to participate.

Medicare Part D is a federal program to subsidize the costs of prescription drugs for Medicare beneficiaries in the United States. The benefit is administered by private insurance plans that are then reimbursed by the **Centers for Medicare and Medicaid Services** (CMS). Beneficiaries can obtain the Medicare drug benefit through two types of private plans: they can join a **Prescription Drug Plan** (PDP) for drug coverage only or they can join a **Medicare Advantage plan** (MA) that covers both medical services and prescription drugs (MA-PD). Those who enroll in the Medicare Part D program choose from a long list of approved drug plans, which do not cover all prescription drugs, so it is important that they choose a plan that meets their needs.

Medigap or Medicare Supplemental Insurance is intended to complement, not replace, Medicare as a primary means of coverage. The supplement provides payment for additional benefits not covered. Most of these policies pay substantially less than the cost of the expenses not covered under Medicare. Insurance companies that sell Medigap policies are required by law to have an open enrollment period of six months for those individuals who first enroll in Medicare Part B at age 65 or older. Insurance companies can, however, exclude pre-existing conditions from the data of initial coverage, but for no more than six months. Each policy is mandated to provide a basic amount of benefits.

Medicare Explanation of Benefits

Source:
http://www.medicare.gov/Basics/SummaryNotice_HowToReadB.asp

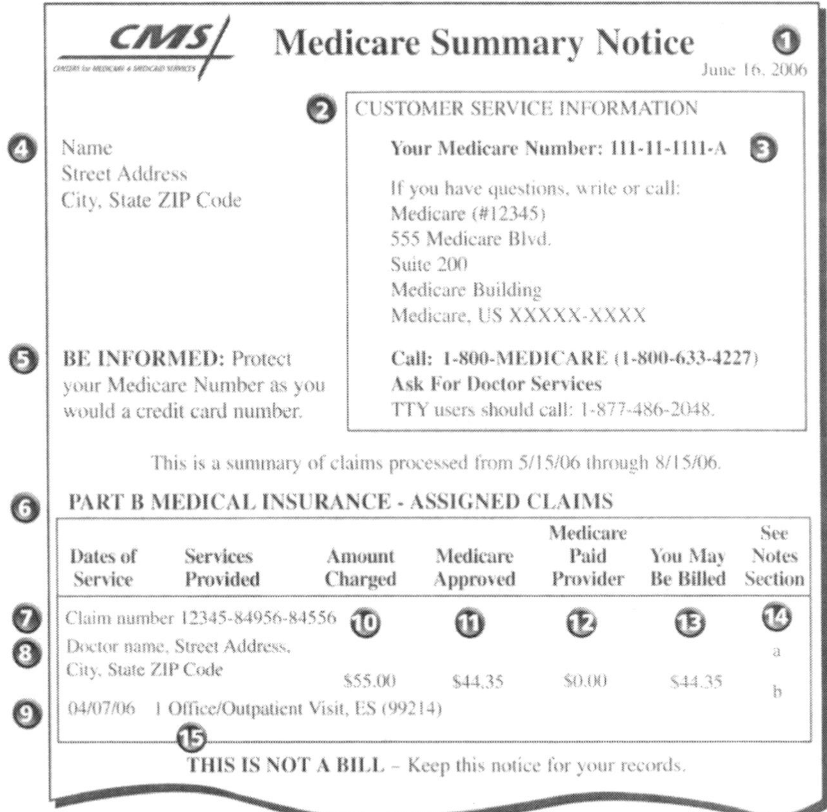

CMS

Medicare Summary Notice (1)

June 16, 2006

(2) CUSTOMER SERVICE INFORMATION

Your Medicare Number: 111-11-1111-A (3)

If you have questions, write or call:
Medicare (#12345)
555 Medicare Blvd.
Suite 200
Medicare Building
Medicare, US XXXXX-XXXX

Call: 1-800-MEDICARE (1-800-633-4227)
Ask For Doctor Services
TTY users should call: 1-877-486-2048.

(4) Name
Street Address
City, State ZIP Code

(5) **BE INFORMED:** Protect your Medicare Number as you would a credit card number.

This is a summary of claims processed from 5/15/06 through 8/15/06.

(6) **PART B MEDICAL INSURANCE - ASSIGNED CLAIMS**

Dates of Service	Services Provided	Amount Charged	Medicare Approved	Medicare Paid Provider	You May Be Billed	See Notes Section
(7) Claim number 12345-84956-84556		(10)	(11)	(12)	(13)	(14)
(8) Doctor name, Street Address, City, State ZIP Code		$55.00	$44.35	$0.00	$44.35	a
(9) 04/07/06	1 Office/Outpatient Visit, ES (99214)					b

(15)

THIS IS NOT A BILL - Keep this notice for your records.

1. **Date:** Date Medicare Summary Notice (MSN) was sent.

2. **Customer Service Information:** Who to contact with questions about the MSN. Provide your Medicare number (3), the date of the MSN (1) and the date of the service you have a question about (9).

3. **Medicare Number:** The number on your Medicare card.

4. **Name and Address:** If incorrect, contact both the company listed in (2) and the Social Security Administration immediately.

5. **Be Informed:** Messages about ways to protect yourself and Medicare from fraud and abuse.

6. **Part B Medical Insurance - Assigned Claims:** Type of service. See the back of MSN for information about assignment. (**Please Note:** For unassigned services, this section is called "**Part B Medical Insurance - Unassigned Claims.**")

7. **Claim Number:** Number that identifies this specific claim.

8. **Provider's Name and Address:** Doctor (may show clinic, group and/or referring doctor) or provider's name and billing address. The referring doctor's name may also be shown if the service was ordered or referred by another doctor. The address shown is the billing address, which may be different from where you physically received the services.

9. **Dates of Service:** Date your service or supply was received. You may use these dates to compare with the dates shown on the bill you receive from your doctor.

10. **Amount Charged:** Amount the provider billed Medicare.

11. **Medicare Approved:** Amount Medicare approves for this service or supply.

12. **Medicare Paid Provider:** Amount Medicare has already paid to the provider. (**Please Note:** For unassigned services, this column is called "**Medicare Paid You.**")

13. **You May Be Billed:** The total amount the provider may bill you, including deductibles, coinsurance and non-covered charges. Medicare supplement (Medigap) policies may pay all or part of this amount.

14. **See Notes Section:** If letter appears, refer to (16) on the next page for explanation.

15. **Services Provided:** Brief description of the service or supply received.

16 **Notes Section:**

a This information is being sent to your private insurer(s). Send any questions regarding your benefits to them.

b This approved amount has been applied toward your deductible.

17 **Deductible Information:**

You have now met $44.35 of your $100 Part B deductible for 2006.

18 **General Information:**

Please notify us if your address has changed or is incorrect as shown on this notice.

19 **Appeals Information - Part B**

If you disagree with any claims decisions on this notice, your appeal must be received by **November 1, 2006**.

Follow the instructions below:

1) Circle the item(s) you disagree with and explain why you disagree.

2) Send this notice, or a copy, to the address in the "Customer Service Information" box on Page 1.

3) Sign here____________________Phone Number (___)____________

16. **Notes Section:** Explains letters in (14) for more detailed information about your claim.
17. **Deductible Information:** How much of your yearly deductible you have met.
18. **General Information:** Important Medicare news and information.
19. **Appeals Information:** How and when to request an appeal.

Medicaid

Just as Medicare aims to aid a population with limited resources and income, Medicaid works on the same premise. However, the programs are very different. Medicaid focuses on individuals and families with low incomes and limited resources that fall into specific Eligibility Groups (unlike Medicare which is an entitlement program for all seniors 65 and older) which may contain guidelines associated with age, whether you are pregnant, disabled or blind. Guidelines also include income assessment and United States citizenship review. These requirements often vary from group to group and state to state.

Medicaid was created in 1965 as a supplement to the Social Security Act. Unlike Medicare, the federal government and state governments jointly fund Medicaid. Participation in the program is voluntary, however all states have participated since 1982. Each state is responsible for setting their eligibility and services guidelines for the program while the **Centers for Medicare and Medicaid Services (CMS)** help to oversee the programs and distribute money to states that meet federal guidelines for matching funds and grants.

State "Titled" Programs

State sponsored Medicaid programs are often given unique titles such as "Tenn-Care," "Medi-Cal" and "MassHealth." So remember when searching for the program that "Medicaid" may not be in the title.

If your income is low and you think you may be eligible for Medicaid – apply. Each state has qualified social workers to review your individual case and/or assess your family's medical needs. Just remember that low income is not the only qualifier for a Medicaid program. You must also fall within one of the Eligibility Groups. To find out more information about the Medicaid program and Eligibility Groups visit the U.S. Department of Health and Human Services website at **http://www.cms.hhs.gov/medicaideligibility/**.

TRICARE

TRICARE is the civilian health program for all active duty service members, National Guard and Reserve members, retirees, families and dependents. There are approximately 9 million individuals eligible for TRICARE benefits. And for many individuals TRICARE ends up functioning as a secondary insurance. Similar to other government healthcare programs, there are eligibility requirements for enrollment. First and foremost, you must be registered in the Defense Enrollment Eligibility Reporting System (DEERS), a database holding records for service members, their families, retirees and others eligible for military benefits. TRICARE then offers several different health plans including **TRICARE Prime**, **TRICARE Standard** and **TRICARE Extra**, along with two dental plan options and special programs which include health promotion and clinical trials.

Other Resources

The site run by the **Centers for Medicare & Medicaid Services** is part of the federal government's Health and Human Services. It is the site for all things related to Medicare and Medicaid and can be found at **www.CMS.gov** or **www.CMS.HHS.gov**

You can specifically find information on **Medicaid**, mandatory and optional Eligibility Groups and income/resource guidelines by visiting **http://www.cms.hhs.gov/home/medicaid.asp**

Information on **TRICARE** plans, eligibility guidelines and enrollment visit **http://tricare.mil/mybenefit/index.jsp**

8

FINAL RANT

The Disenfranchising of the American Healthcare Consumer

We call it the all-you-can-eat healthcare buffet, but how does healthcare stack up to a dining experience? Both are very personal experiences. But **Patsy Kelly** of **Medical Bill Review Services Inc.** (www.MedBillReview.com) offers this interesting analogy; in a restaurant, you decide what food to order, you consume the food and then pay for the food and service. In healthcare, the patient does not order the service or have primary responsibility for payment. Additionally, the person who pays for the service does not order it or consume it, and the person who orders it does not pay for it or consume it.

Now we all know and agree that a patient should not be ordering their own healthcare tests and services. However, there is still a disconnect between delivery and consumption here. Even the person who orders and delivers the care typically is unaware of its costs.

Let's try to imagine a restaurant set up like our healthcare system; first you really didn't choose the restaurant, someone else suggested it – your insurer. You didn't place your order – your doctor or a specialist did. You ate the food. But you didn't pay for the food – your insurer did. Was it good? Did it satisfy? Was it fairly priced? Did you overpay? How was the service? Would you go back? Do you have a choice?

Feeling disenfranchised yet?

They Bill Us and We Pay Them

I went to a specialist and he breezed me through. I felt rushed because he was. But he had been recommended by my primary care physician, so I accepted the situation. They collected images for my insurance to get authorization, did a scan and sent me home to wait. They would call when they got pre-authorization for the procedure.

The nurse called. The images had not been satisfactory for my insurer. They needed me to come back.

"So, who pays for this?" I asked.

The nurse clearly was not prepared for the question, but to her credit she recovered quickly and responded that it was not my error, and they had apparently not been thorough enough with the images. There would be no charge.

So, I went.

The business office receptionist asked for my co-pay. I explained the situation, and she looked very confused.

"I don't know how to do this without a co-pay." Finally, she figured it out.

I got the images remade and went home.

Then I got the bill and subsequently the statement. My insurance had paid $49. I still owed $20, the co-pay. So, I called. They reviewed it and sent me another statement stating that I still owed $20 and that my insurance had paid their $49 portion.

I called my insurer and explained that there should not have been a bill. I told customer service.

"They bill us. We pay them," I was told.

I explained that those were my premium dollars they had paid. The second trip was the doctor's responsibility – the doctor's nurse had told me it was.

She told me, "That is a private agreement between you and your doctor. We have a contract that they bill us, and we pay them."

I called the provider back again and asked for another review. I got it. This time they agreed to waive the $20 co-pay fee, but they kept the $49 that the insurer had paid.

- Robert Hendrick
change:healthcare

Becoming a Responsible Consumer

As Americans we have become displaced from the healthcare process. This outcome has been accomplished slowly and methodically by a number of market forces. The healthcare consumer exercises a small degree of choice in which provider they visit, but without the proper information, how can they make the right choice? There is no clearly-priced menu at the door. There is no quality score posted for consumers to view. It's only $20, we tell ourselves. It's no wonder that we've become disenfranchised by the healthcare process.

Americans have finally begun to wake up to the issues regarding their health. And healthcare is the hot topic among politicians as well as employers and even healthcare providers.

Restaurants are trying to provide healthy food and information about the costs of eating. Menus no longer describe just the price, but also the quality of the food – how many calories, how many grams of fat, grams of sugar. Some states (like New York, for example) are even beginning to ban trans fats in

Consumers Are Driving Change

Thanks to the Internet, we all have new power. We have a voice. We have new tools. We have wisdom at our fingertips. Every patient, every caregiver, every doctor, every entrepreneur, every person can now make a difference and can now manage their healthcare in a way like never before.

We can't afford to wait around anymore for politicians to fix this system. Luckily, consumers are quickly gaining more control. Every one of us. We're now living in a world of consumer-driven healthcare and it's up to us to change the system.

How do we do this? We must arm ourselves with knowledge, wisdom and information. Demand transparency in pricing by researching alternatives. Negotiate! Take control of your own healthcare now. The more you know, the more power you have.

-Unity Stoakes
OrganizedWisdom.com

restaurant cuisine. Getting that information at a restaurant was unheard of only a few years ago, but a combined effort of public outcry along with government-backed prodding finally got the restaurant industry to step into line.

Healthcare needs the same sort of transparency that the food industry has opened itself up to. That comes down to the three "C's" we talked about earlier:

- Cost
- Conversation
- Quality

We as Americans need to understand the costs of healthcare. We need to open up and have candid conversations about healthcare without fear of judgment. And we need to have quality measures so we can make the decisions about what aspect of a provider is most important to us.

The more we all understand about the system and how it truly works, the more we take back control and become the responsible healthcare consumers we should be – and the better our chances of surviving this system.

Other Resources

SHOUTAmerica is a non-profit, non-partisan organization that encourages people to develop and implement sustainable solutions to the impending health care crisis through awareness, education and the promotion of dialogue. Of several paramount issues facing the future of this nation, the rising cost of health care has the ability to simultaneously jeopardize the economic stability of our government, our businesses and the American people themselves. Therefore SHOUTAmerica seeks to bring together and educate America's youth, who stand to shoulder the greatest consequences if long-term, comprehensive reform is not achieved. By empowering their voices, SHOUTAmerica will encourage young Americans to actively take responsibility for their future and address the challenges of healthcare head on. For more information visit **www.SHOUTAmerica.com**

The **Cover America Tour**, sponsored by Consumer Reports Health, is traveling across the country to hear your healthcare story – all in an effort to make sure politicians listen to what Americans are saying about our broken system. For more information, videos or to follow the tour check them out at **www.CoverAmericaTour.org**

My Healthcare Is Killing Me has its very own website. For reviews of the book, personal healthcare stories and more, visit **www.myhealthcareiskillingme.com**

GLOSSARY

-A-

Adjusted Gross Income is an income figure computed when calculating taxes. It is based on gross income, less any business expenses and deductions like retirement account contributions or alimony. Itemized deductions, such as medical expenses, interest payments and real estate taxes, are included in the adjusted gross income calculation and not subtracted out until "net taxable income" is determined.

Adjustment (see Network Discount)

Allied Practitioner is a professionally degreed healthcare service provider other than a Physician M.D.

Allowed Amount is the amount of payment a provider has agreed to accept for a service, treatment or product under the terms of a negotiated contract with an insurer (also Adjusted Amount, Allowed Bill, Allowed Rate, Negotiated Rate)

Amount Applied to Deductible is the amount of money considered to be the patient responsibility which is credited against the deductible in a healthcare plan.

Amount Not Covered (see Non-Covered Charges)

-B-

Balance is the amount remaining from a debt once all existing payments and adjustments have been considered.

Bill is the paperwork received from a provider which documents the services rendered and shows the gross amount billed for those services. This amount should match the claim amount submitted to the insurer (see also super bill).

Billed Amount is the amount initially billed by a provider for a service, treatment or product.

Billing Date is the date on which a bill was issued.

-C-

CDHP (see Consumer Directed Healthcare Plan)

CPT (see Current Procedural Terminology)

Capitated Contract refers to a contract between an insurer and a provider under which the provider agrees to accept set amounts for products and services rendered to those individuals under the insurer's policy.

Caregiver is a person responsible for the well-being of a patient. Generally a family member or close companion.

Centers for Medicare and Medicaid Services (CMS) is the title of a federal agency within the United States Department of Health and Human Services. CMS is responsible for administering Medicare and works with state governments to administer Medicaid and the State Children's Health Insurance Program.

Chronic Condition (also referred to as Chronic Disease) describes a medical condition which is persistent and long-lasting. A chronic condition is consistently present and requires managed care. Multiple Sclerosis, diabetes, hypertension and heart disease are examples of chronic conditions.

Claim is a request for reimbursement submitted to an insurer by a provider in anticipation of receiving payment for covered services rendered by that provider.

Claim Number is a unique identifier number assigned to a claim by an insurer.

Clinic is a licensed facility where healthcare services are rendered to patients.

Co-Insurance represents the percentage split of the healthcare cost responsibility between the insurer and insured in relation to insurance coverage after the deductible has been met. For example, on an 80/20 co-insurance plan, the insurance company will cover 80% of the cost and the patient will be responsible for the remaining 20%.

Co-Pay (also Co-Payment) is a fixed amount that an insured patient is expected to pay out-of-pocket at the time of service.

Co-Payment (see Co-Pay)

Coordination of Benefits refers to the management, collection and reporting of claims for individuals covered by more than one insurance plan. This coordination helps to ensure that maximum benefit and payments have been made on the insured's behalf.

Collection Notice is a notice received that demands payment of overdue debt for a bill(s).

Consumer Directed Healthcare Plan (or CDHP) is a healthcare plan in which the consumer directs and is responsible for payment up to the generally higher deductible amount. The insurer accepts payment responsibility only after that obligation has been reached by the consumer.

Contracted Amount (see Allowed Amount)

Coverage is the defined scope of services provided under a specific healthcare policy.

Current Procedural Terminology (more commonly known as **CPT)** are the codes used by physicians to communicate a medical, surgical or diagnostic service primarily for the purpose of submitting a claim for reimbursement of the service.

-D-

DRG (see **Diagnosis Related Groups**)

Denial of Coverage is the refusal of an insurer to accept responsibility as the guaranteed payor for services, treatments or products considered to be outside the scope of a defined healthcare plan.

Dental refers to preventative healthcare related to the teeth.

Diagnosis Related Groups (more commonly known as **DRG**) is a code used by hospitals primarily for the purpose of prospective reimbursement. The codes help to classify cases and patients who are treated with similar hospital services.

Disallowed Charges (see Non-Covered Charges)

Disease Management is the proactive management of health issues in an effort to reduce healthcare costs and improve quality of life for patients with chronic diseases.

Donut Hole is slang for the phase of a Medicare enrollee's pharmaceutical plan under the Medicare Part D prescription drug program during which costs are not covered by Medicare.

-E-

EOB (see Explanation of Benefits)

ERISA (see Employee Retirement Income Security Act)

Employee Retirement Income Security Act is a federal law enacted in 1974 that places responsibility for the oversight of insurers at the state level unless a company is self-funded in which case responsibility falls under the federal government.

Excluded Amount (see Non-Covered Charges)

Excluded Expenses (see Non-Covered Charges)

Explanation of Benefits (or EOB) is a patient's documentation of a claim and the allocation of financial responsibility for that claim. An EOB is specific to a provider and the service(s) rendered by that provider. The format varies widely between insurers, but at a minimum should indicate the Provider, Service Date, Actual Billed Amount, Network Discount, Allowed Amount, Insurance Portion, Patient Responsibility and Deductible Amount.

-F-

FSA (see Flexible Spending Account)

Filed By is either the provider or the patient. This option designates whether the provider submits the claim to the insurer or the patient submits the claim to the insurer.

Flexible Spending Account (or FSA) is generally an employer-funded or individual-funded account that receives pre-tax dollars and can be used for a multitude of personally related expenses that are tax-deductible including childcare and healthcare.

Family Member is, for the purpose of an insurer, a spouse or child (natural, adopted or otherwise legally bound) under a specified age depending on insurer requirements in compliance with state and federal laws. Legislation in your state may impact the definition of a spouse or family member.

-G-

Gatekeeper is a primary care physician through whom a patient receives a referral to a specialist.

Guaranteed Payor is an entity which, under contract, pledges payment for services, treatments or product.

-H-

HDHP (see High Deductible Healthcare Plan)

HIPAA (see Healthcare Information Portability and Accountability Act)

HMO (see Healthcare Maintenance/Management Organization)

HRA (see Healthcare Reimbursement Account)

HSA (see Healthcare Savings Account)

Healthcare Information Portability and Accountability Act is federal legislation regarding patient's rights with respect to the handling and privacy of an individual's healthcare records by healthcare industry professionals.

Healthcare Maintenance/Management Organization is a type of Managed Care Organization (MCO) that provides a form of health insurance coverage fulfilled through hospitals, doctors and other providers with which the HMO has a contract.

Health Reimbursement Accounts (or HRAs) are IRS-approved arrangements between the employer and employee where healthcare expenses are reimbursed to the employee after initial payment. Only pre-approved healthcare expenses are reimbursed by the employer.

Healthcare Savings Account (or Healthcare Spending Account) is a savings account associated with a high deductible health plan (HDHP) that receives pre-tax dollars, from which the consumer pays their deductible and other related health expenses.

Healthcare Spending Account (see Healthcare Savings Account)

High Deductible Healthcare Plan is (HDHP or CDHP) is a health insurance plan with lower premiums and higher deductibles than a traditional health plan. It is sometimes referred to as a consumer directed health plan. Participating in a "qualified" HDHP is a requirement for

Health Savings Accounts and other tax-advantaged programs.

Hospital is an institution for healthcare, either for profit or not-for-profit, which provides treatment to patients. Many hospitals have specialized staff and equipment to handle unique medical occurrences and emergencies.

-I-

ICD (see International Classification of Diseases)

Income Tax is federal tax on earnings and wages.

Ineligible Amount (see Non-Covered Charges)

In-Network refers to providers who are contracted with an individual's insurer to provide services at a pre-determined rate. Most insurers maintain a negotiated contract with the providers commonly used by their insured. Many of these contracts are regionally confined since insurers are authorized on a state-by-state basis as a result of ERISA.

Insurance Portion is the amount that your insurance company pays on a claim.

Insurer is a guaranteed payor authorized on a state-by-state basis. Insurers act as the agent for a patient to process healthcare claims from a provider. The insurer then makes reimbursements to the provider on behalf of the insured patient.

International Classification of Diseases (more commonly know as **ICD**) is the international standard for communicating global information regarding disease.

-L-

Lab (short for laboratory) is a medical services provider, separate from the physician, which performs clinical tests on bodily tissues and fluids.

-M-

Medicaid is an insurance program that is jointly funded by the states and the federal government, but is administered by each state to provide health care for certain low-income individuals and families in order to reimburse hospitals and physicians for providing care to qualifying people who cannot finance their own medical expenses.

Medical Tax Deduction is an itemized schedule of medical expenses eligible for tax write-off.

Medicare is a social insurance program administered by the United States government which provides health insurance coverage to people who are age 65 and over, or who meet special criteria.

Medicare Advantage plans (MA) are private health plans that receive payment directly from Medicare. These plans offer HMOs, PPOs, provider-sponsored organizations, private fee-for-service plans and high deductible plans. You must be a participant of Medicare Part A and Part B to join a Medicare Advantage Plan.

Medicare Advantage Prescription Drug plan (MA-PD) is a Medicare Advantage plan that also includes prescription drug coverage within a unified single plan.

Medicare HMO (aka **Part C**) is a new designation that permits Medicare recipients to select coverage among various private healthcare plans to include HMOs, PPOs, Point-of-Service (POS), Medical Savings Accounts (MSAs), fee-for-service plans and provider-sponsored plans..

Medicare Part D prescription drug program (or Medicare Part D – see also Donut Hole) is a federal government program meant to subsidize the costs of prescription drugs for Medicare beneficiaries in the United States.

Medicare Supplemental (aka **Medigap Insurance**) is an insurance policy designed to act as a supplement to Medicare.

Medigap (see Medicare Supplemental)

Mileage is the distance traveled in a personal vehicle for the purpose of receiving healthcare treatment or services.

-N-

NDC (see National Drug Code)

Named Insured is the person through whom a health insurance policy is secured. For an employer-sponsored plan, that would be the employee.

National Drug Code is an identifying code unique to each drug and its dosage. It has a standardized three-part format. The three segments represent the labeler code, the product code and the package code.

Negotiated Rate/Amount (see Allowed Amount)

Network Discount is the amount by which a provider's bill is adjusted as a result of a negotiated rate agreed upon between the provider and the insurer. This network discount term often appears on an Explanation of Benefits, but forms may vary by insurer. Insurers use many variations on this term including adjustment, discount and provider discount.

Non-Covered Charges are expenses associated with a claim that has been denied or charges that exceed the allowed amount. Non-covered charges are often associated with a reason code which classifies and explains why these charges have been denied or excluded. (see Excluded Expenses, Excluded Amount, Amount Not Covered, Ineligible Amount or Disallowed Charges)

-O-

Out-of-Network refers to providers who are not directly contracted with an individual's insurer to deliver products or services at a pre-determined rate. Most insurers maintain a negotiated contract with the providers commonly used by their insured. Many of these contracts are regionally confined since insurers are generally regionally constrained.

OTC (see Over-the-Counter)

Out-of Pocket is the amount personally paid by the insured patient for incurred healthcare expenses.

Over-the-Counter (or OTC) is any drug not requiring a prescription for purchase. Usually these drugs can be found on the shelves of any drug or discount store.

-P-

PCP (see Primary Care Physician)

PPO (see Preferred Provider Organization)

POS (see Point-of-Service)

Participating Provider is a provider who has agreed under a contract with an insurer to accept patients from a insurance plan.

Patient is the individual receiving care.

Patient Advocate is a person who speaks for the patient in instances where the patient lacks the subject matter knowledge or is otherwise unable to communicate effectively without assistance.

Patient Responsibility is the portion of the provider charges to be paid by the patient.

Payment Method is the means by which a payment was made (i.e. cash, check, credit card, etc.)

Payor is the entity (company or individual) making payment on an outstanding debt.

Pharmacy is a retail-based establishment where pharmaceutical prescriptions, other medications and medical devices are dispensed.

Physical Therapist is a healthcare professional concerned with prevention, treatment and management of movement disorders arising from conditions, diseases and injuries occurring throughout the lifespan of a particular patient.

Physician is any type of medical practitioner who holds an advanced degree in medicine, usually specializing in a specific body field or function. Physicians are degreed as Medical Doctor (M.D.) or Doctor of Osteopathy (D.O.).

Policy is a contract between the insured and an insurer detailing which services are covered by the insurer.

Policy Holder is a person covered under an insurance policy.

Point of Service Plan (or **POS**) offers an approved network of medical care facilities and physicians for their policy holders to choose from just like an HMO or a PPO. A major difference is that point-of-service plans allow for their policy holders to receive their medical care outside of the network, though use of facilities and physicians within the network is encouraged.

Practitioner is anyone licensed to provide healthcare services.

Pre-Authorization is the confirmation of coverage for a service or product by the insurer prior to the rendering of the service or disbursement of the product by the provider.

Pre-Tax Account holds money, which is available for certain eligible expenses and will not be subject to the deduction of state or federal income tax.

Premium is the amount paid for an insurance coverage. Premiums are usually paid on a pay period or monthly basis.

Preferred Provider Organization (or **PPO**) is a managed care organization of medical doctors, hospitals and other healthcare providers who have contracted with an insurer or a third-party administrator to provide healthcare at reduced rates to the insurer's or administrator's clients.

Prescription is a physician-approved authorization for the distribution and consumption of a controlled pharmaceutical or product.

Prescription Drug Plan (or **PDP)** is a network of pharmacies contracted to an insurance plan to provide pharmaceutical services for their insured. The plan usually includes co-payments for drugs, with varying payment amounts based on whether the drug is generic or name brand.

Primary Care Physician (or **PCP**) is a physician selected within an HMO plan as the professional who will act as the coordinator for patient care and be responsible for approving or denying referral requests. PCPs are usually indicated by titles such as Internal Medicine, General Practitioners, Family Practice or Pediatricians.

Primary Insurance is the first insurer when more than one insurance policy provides concurrent coverage. The primary insurance often sets the allowed amount that a provider is able to bill. There is a coordination of benefits that must take place when there is more than one insurance in effect. Benefits from a primary insuror must be completed before submitting a claim to a secondary insuror.

Private Insurance is insurance provided through an entity either for-profit or not-for-profit, and other than the federal or state government.

Privatized Healthcare is healthcare coverage not provided by the state or federal government.

Promissory Note is an agreement which documents and binds an obligation to pay back a specified amount of money to an individual or group.

Provider is anyone who provides medically related services that can be reimbursed. A provider may be a physician, nurse, dentist, clinic, hospital, pharmacy, lab, physical therapist or other allied practitioner.

Provider Accepts Adjustment is a term referring to the fact that a provider has settled on a negotiated rate with an insurer.

-R-

RBC (see Retail-Based Clinic)

Reason for Visit is the condition or symptom that prompted a patient to engage a provider. The reason for visit is a plain language means for the layperson to interpret a condition (see also CPT code).

Referral is a recommendation by a primary care physician to visit a specialist or move from one specialist to another specialist.

Reimbursement is the transfer of a payment made for services rendered. Reimbursement may be made to a provider or to a patient in the event that overpayment has been made or the patient pre-paid and submitted for reimbursement consideration directly from their insurer.

Retail-Based Clinics (or **RBC**) are non-acute care providers based in retail establishments such as pharmacies, department stores and grocery stores for the purpose of convenience.

-S-

SCHIP is the **State Children's Health Insurance Program** (SCHIP), a United States federal government program that gives funds to states in order to provide health insurance to families with children. The program was designed to cover uninsured children in families with incomes that are modest but still too high to qualify for Medicaid.

Sandwich Generation is a slang term identifying the group of adults who have the responsibility for care of both their own children and their elderly parents.

Secondary Insurance is an insurance which provides coverage in addition to that of a primary insurance. Secondary insurance generally covers services not covered or not completely covered by the primary insurance. When a person has a secondary insurance or even a tertiary insurance, there must be coordination of benefits.

Self-Funded refers to a company which funds their health insurance plan and pays for claims with their own money. The amount of money needed to pay for claims is estimated by insurance actuaries and set aside to pay for healthcare expenses.

Self-Pay is payment for service solely by the patient.

Service (as relates to a provider) is the procedure of product rendered by a provider to a patient such as a physician visit, radiology services or laboratory services.

Service Date is the date on which a medical service was rendered by a provider.

Specialty is a provider's specific area of expertise.

Specialist is a medical professional with concentrated expertise in a specific field of medicine (i.e. oncology, podiatry, etc.). (See also specialty)

Statement is a summary of all outstanding activity on an open account balance.

Super Bill is a term for a more extensive line item documentation of a bill from a provider.

-T-

TPA (see Third-Party Administrator)

Tags are keywords that are used to group records into categories for organization.

Tax-Deductible is a term referring to expenses which are legally excluded from federal income tax.

Tertiary Insurance is the third insuror when three instances of an insured's coverage are concurrently in effect. See also primary insurance, secondary insurance and coordination of benefits.

Third-Party Administrator (or **TPA**) is an organization contracted with either an insurance provider or an employer to carry out the functions of claims processing, physician network management and often referral/utilization review.

Transaction Log is a sortable list of all financial activity within an account.

TRICARE is the United States military managed healthcare program for the military, dependents and retirees and replaced the previous CHAMPUS plan. The program is managed by TRICARE Management Activity (TMA) and contracts with several large health insurance corporations to provide claims processing, customer service and other administrative functions. There are three different TRICARE plans (see below).

TRICARE Standard provides a similar benefit to the original CHAMPUS program. Beneficiaries can use any civilian health care provider that is payable under TRICARE regulations. The beneficiary is responsible for payment of an annual deductible and coinsurance, and may be responsible for certain other out-of-pocket expenses. There is no open enrollment in TRICARE Standard.

TRICARE Extra allows Standard beneficiaries to elect to use a civilian healthcare provider from within the regional contractor's provider network. TRICARE Extra represents a preferred provider organization (PPO), and the beneficiary's coinsurance amount is reduced by at least five percentage points.

TRICARE Prime is administered in a health maintenance organization (HMO) plan format. Beneficiaries must choose a primary care physician and obtain referrals and authorizations for specialty care.

-U-

Underinsured describes someone with financial strain resulting from inadequate insurance coverage to address the financial expenses associated with healthcare services.

Uninsured describes someone without health insurance coverage.

-V-

Vision refers to portions of a policy that cover basic eye care including regular checkups and a regular stipend for the purchase of corrective lenses or contacts.

-W-

Will Bill is a designation that notes whether a patient should expect to receive a bill for services. There may be situations where the prior payment serves as the bill (i.e. a pharmacy purchase).

ABOUT THE AUTHORS

Robert Hendrick

Robert is one of the co-founders of change:healthcare, located in Nashville, Tennessee. *My Healthcare Is Killing Me* is his first non-fiction effort. His entire career has been spent finding ways to use technology to make information more easily accessible with a great deal of focus on healthcare. Robert holds an undergraduate degree from Auburn University in Auburn, Alabama and a master's degree from The Ohio State University in Columbus, Ohio. He lives in Nashville, Tennessee with his wife Sally and three daughters, Kate, Zoe and Annie.

Christopher Parks

Christopher is one of the co-founders of change:healthcare, located in Nashville, Tennessee. He has over seventeen years of experience in healthcare, supply chain and technology sales, operations and consulting. Overwhelmed by the healthcare system and all its problems after both of his parents died of cancer within a year of one another, he began working to create change:healthcare. He now realizes his vision to help others everyday through his work. He currently lives in Franklin, Tennessee with his wife Meredith and two sons, William and Andrew.

Katrina Welty

Katrina is the second employee at change:healthcare and an important part of the moral compass of the company. She holds a double bachelor's degree in Medicine, Health, and Society (an interdisciplinary major combining multiple subjects/departments) and Philosophy from Vanderbilt University. She is interested in finding solutions for the uninsured and simplifying healthcare to enable consumers to make better decisions. In her free time, she enjoys cooking and taking her dog Piper to the park.

ABOUT change:healthcare

change:healthcare, inc. (www.changehealthcare.com) is a technology firm dedicated to helping people become smarter healthcare consumers. The company provides access to a wealth of healthcare information, as well as Internet-based solutions including its medical bill management platform. Their solutions that educate, encourage and reward savvy healthcare consumers are available online directly to individuals, employers, third-party administrators, healthcare providers and medical bill adjudicators.

The company also boasts a core of dedicated bloggers who cover the most current topics related to the American healthcare consumer.

Printed in the United States
130215LV00001B/145/P

9 780981 917252